Kid's Box

New Generation

T0384666

Caroline Nixon &
Michael Tomlinson

CAMBRIDGE

Student's Book
with eBook

American English

5

Language summary

	Key vocabulary	**Key language**	**Sounds and life skills**

Welcome to our blog
page 4

School subjects: *art, computer studies, English, French, geography, German, history, math, music, P.E., science, Spanish*

School: *class, competition, dictionary, language, prize, study, subject, test*

Like/Love + *-ing*/nouns, *I'd like* + infinitive

Simple present questions and short answers: *Do you live near your school? Yes, I do. / No, I don't.*

Connected speech

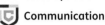 Communication

---

1 Time for TV
page 10

The time: *after, half, o'clock, past, quarter, to*

TV shows: *action movie, cartoon, comedy, documentary, news, quiz show, rock music video, sports, weather*

TV: *channel, episode, series, stream, turn on*

Adjectives: *amazing, bad, boring, exciting, funny, good, interesting*

The time: *What time is it? It's quarter after one.*

Consonant clusters
sh and *ch*
(*finish, channel*)

 Collaboration

Media: How can we make nature documentaries?   page 16

---

2 People at work
page 18

Jobs: *actor, artist, cook, dentist, doctor, mechanic, nurse, pilot, reporter, soccer player, sports commentator, video game designer, writer*

Plans, intentions, and predictions with *going to*: *What's William going to be when he grows up? He's going to be a designer.*

The /ər/ sound
(*doctor*)

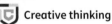 Creative thinking

---

Social studies: How can we stay safe?   page 24

Review units 1 and 2   page 26

---

3 City life
page 28

City life: *airport, bridge, castle, fire station, gym, hotel, movie theater, museum, playground, police station, post office, prison, restaurant, road, stadium, street, taxi, zoo*

Directions: *across, corner, left, past, right, straight ahead, straight down*

Directions: *Go across/past/ straight ahead/straight down, Take the first/second/third street, Turn left/right into/at/on the corner*

Prepositions: *behind, between, next to, across from*

Consonant clusters
str, st, and *sp*
(*street, stadium, sports*)

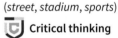 Critical thinking

---

Geography: What are the best modes of transportation?   page 34

---

4 Disaster!
page 36

Disasters: *earthquake, hurricane, iceberg, lightning, storm, tsunami, volcano*

Verbs: *break (a leg), catch fire, cut, destroy, drop, erupt, fall down, hit, hurt, lose*

Months

Past progressive and simple past: *I was having a picnic when it started to rain. What were you doing?*

The vowel sounds
(*sailing, me, sky, hello, rescue*)

 Creative thinking

Geography and history: Where can we find volcanoes?   page 42

Review units 3 and 4   page 44

2

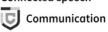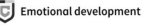

Welcome to our blog

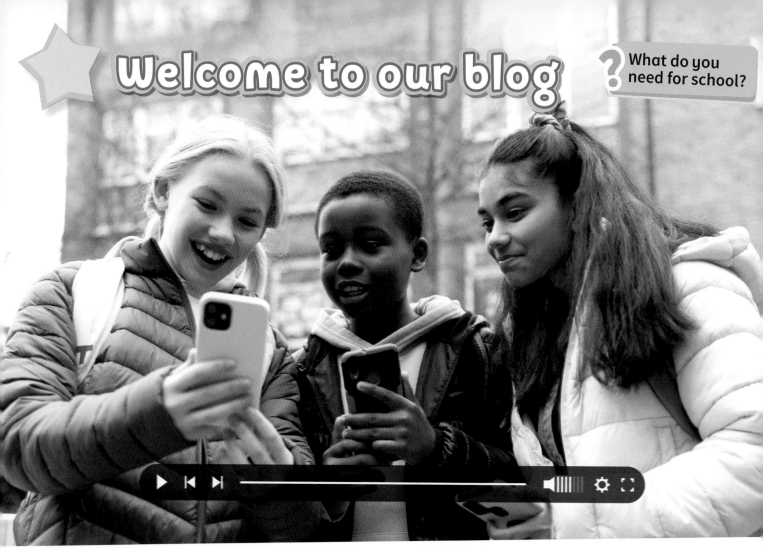

 Who gets an exciting message? Watch and check.

 Watch again. Order.

1 Can we write about sports and technology?
2 Let's meet outside school at four o'clock.
3 Well, it's our first day back at school, so let's write about that.
4 Did you have a good vacation?
5 It's about a new school blog.
6 Are you ready for a new school year?

(Order box: 1)

STUDY

How are things?
Are you ready for a new school year?
Can we write about sports?

 Answer the questions.

1 What are the children's names?
2 Why wasn't Eva online?
3 Where are they?

4 What's the competition for?
5 Why are they excited about the competition?
6 What can they write about?

 Ask and answer.

1 What did you think of Eva's idea for a blog post about their first day at school?
2 Imagine you are writing a blog post for a competition. What would you like to write about?

Language: simple present questions and short answers

Can you remember the last lesson? Watch the language video.

 Read and answer.

All about us

Kid's Box is an exciting new blog for young people. Eva, Sally, and Robert want to write a post for the blog. They all go to the same school. It's called "City School."

Eva

I'm ten. I live near the school, so I walk every day. I have lunch at school with my friends. I love drawing and taking pictures, so I want to put my pictures in the blog and write about the natural world.

Sally

I'm ten. I live in the country outside of town, so I catch a bus to school every morning. I like singing and music, and I enjoy playing the piano. I love reading and studying. I'd like to write about music and science in the blog.

Robert

I'm eleven years old. I always ride my bike to school. I sometimes have breakfast with the school breakfast club before my classes. I love playing soccer and basketball. I'm also interested in computers. I'd like to write about sports and technology in the blog.

1 What's *Kid's Box*?
2 What school do they go to?
3 What does Eva love doing?
4 How old is Sally?
5 What would Sally like to write about?
6 How does Robert go to school?
7 Who's interested in technology?
8 Who's the oldest: Eva, Sally, or Robert?

 Listen and say the name.

🎧 1 Who lives near the school?   Eva does.

Ask and answer.   Do you live near your school?   No, I don't.

live / near school
lunch / home
play / musical instrument

like / sports
read / magazines
use / internet

 Write more questions.

Read the blog. What's their favorite subject?

ALL BLOGS   MY BLOG   NEW POST

Kid's Box Reports

For our first blog post, we went around our school to find out more about what we learn.

We all study these school subjects: math, English, science, P.E., art, and computer studies.

Our school

Older students have to study more school **subjects** and take important **tests**.

Science is an important subject, so we study it every day. This year we're learning about plants and the human body.

We study a **second language**. We can choose French, German, or Spanish.

In our **geography classes**, we learn about different people and their countries.

We use the **dictionaries** in the school library to help us understand new words.

The best subject is **history**. We love learning about the past!

We all agree that the best thing about school right now is the blog **competition**. We all want to win that **prize**!

 Read again and say "same" or "different" for your class.

1 At City School, they all study art.
2 Older students take important tests.
3 They can choose a second language.
4 There are dictionaries in the school library.

5 They study science every day.
6 They are learning about plants and the human body.
7 They learn about different people and their countries.
8 They think history is better than geography.

 Ask and answer.

1 Which languages can you learn at school?

> I can learn French at my school.

2 What's your favorite school subject?

> My favorite school subject is English.

3 **Listen and say the subject.**

 1 A lot of people think the capital of Australia is Sydney, but it isn't. It's Canberra.

Geography.

2 Read and choose the right words.

1 We study the past in **science** / **geography** / **history**.

2 French, Spanish, and German are **languages** / **tests** / **sports**.

3 When we don't understand a word, we can use **a book** / **a dictionary** / **art**.

4 We study plants and the human body in **math** / **P.E.** / **science**.

5 We learn about people and countries in **geography** / **computer studies** / **music**.

6 Teachers sometimes find out what we know by giving us **subjects** / **computers** / **tests**.

3 **4–5** Read and write. Listen and check. Do karaoke.

Because school is cool, it's where we go
From Monday to Friday, I'm sure you know.
We study, and we play, that's what we do.
We do it in the morning and the afternoon!

I really love ⁽¹⁾ _____ ,

And I enjoy ⁽²⁾ _____ .

I like to study ⁽³⁾ _____ , too!

My favorite subject in the afternoon.

Before lunch we have ⁽⁴⁾ _____ ,

And then ⁽⁵⁾ _____ ,

And on Wednesday we have ⁽⁶⁾ _____ .

That's a class that is too short!

And I like to do ⁽⁷⁾ _____ ,

Spanish, French, and Japanese.

A lot of words in the ⁽⁸⁾ _____

For me to study and to read.

4 Read about the school words. What are they?

With this subject we can learn to talk to people from another country.
In this class we learn about plants and the human body.
When we study this, we learn about different countries and people.
We use this to learn new words.

5   Write three more definitions. Ask and answer.

With this subject we can learn about numbers and shapes. What is it?

Is it math?

Yes, it is.

Sounds and life skills
Chatting with friends

1 ▶ Watch the video. Where are the young people and how do they feel?

Pronunciation focus

2 🎧 6 **Listen and complete.**

SALLY: Hi, Eva. _____ _____ have a good vacation?

EVA: Yeah, great, thanks.

SALLY: I didn't see you online – _____ _____?

EVA: Because we didn't have wi-fi, but I can show you pictures if you want. Oh, look! Here's Robert!

SALLY: Hi, Robert. _____ _____ things?

ROBERT: Good, thanks, Sally. _____ _____ ready for the new school year?

SALLY: Yeah, _____ _____.

3 🎧 7 **Listen and circle the words that sound connected. Practice with a partner.**

1 (How are) things?
2 Are you happy to be back?
3 Did you have a good summer?

4 In pairs, look at the quiz and add more school vacation activities.

Find out who ...	Extra information	
_____ traveled by train.	Where? _____	Who with? _____
_____ went to a carnival.	Where? _____	What rides? _____
_____ watched a movie.	What movie? _____	Who with? _____
_____ hiked in the country.	Where? _____	Who with? _____
_____ played a lot of sports.	What sports? _____	Who with? _____

Did you have a good vacation?

5 Find a classmate who did each activity. Ask extra questions.

Useful language

How are things?
Where did you go?
Who did you go with?

Sounds and life skills: connected speech | 🛡 communication

Diggory Bones

1 What's Diggory Bones teaching? What's the Baloney Stone?

1 Time for TV

1 **What TV show do they all want to watch? Watch and check.**

2 **Watch again. Say "yes" or "no."**

1 The children are in the supermarket at the beginning of the story.
2 The soccer game is on TV at ten after four.
3 The girls want to watch a show called *Top Talent*.
4 Mr. Sharma wants to watch the same show as them.
5 The golf finishes at twenty to seven.
6 Robert and Sally have to be home at quarter after six.

 No.

STUDY

It's **quarter to** four.
It's **quarter after** four.

3 **Read and match.**

1 The children are in the kitchen   a   at ten after four.
2 The soccer game is on   b   at twenty to seven.
3 *Top Talent* is on   c   at twenty after four.
4 The children arrive in the living room   d   at twenty-five after four.
5 The golf finishes   e   at quarter after four.
6 Robert and Sally have to be home   f   at six thirty.

4 **Ask and answer.**

1 Would you like to watch *Top Talent*? Why? Why not?
2 What do you and your family do when you want to watch different TV shows?

1 ▶ **Can you remember the last lesson? Watch the language video.**

2 **Read and label the clock.** | ten after   five after   twenty-five to   quarter to |

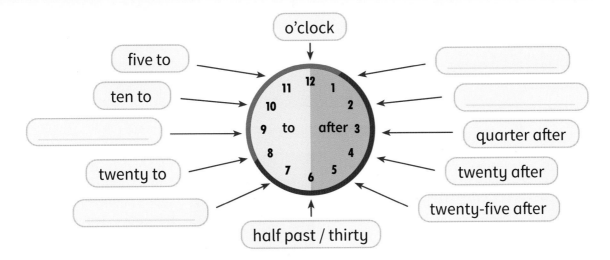

o'clock

five to
ten to
_____
twenty to
_____

half past / thirty

_____
_____
quarter after
twenty after
twenty-five after

3 **What do you do every day? Order.**

wake up		1 brush my teeth	
get up		go to bed	
get dressed		do my homework	
go to school		have breakfast	

4 🎧 9 **Look at the clocks. Listen and say the letter.**

🎧 **1** I have lunch at quarter to one every day.   a

1

3

2

4

5 **Play the game. Ask and answer.**

I get up at this time on Mondays. What time is it?

No.

Yes.

Twenty after seven.

Twenty to eight.

6 **Write about your day. Write 20–30 words.**

1 **Read the blog. Which show is on TV at the same time every day?**

ALL BLOGS   MY BLOG   NEW POST

Kid's Box Reports

Today's blog post is about different kinds of TV shows. You can watch them on TV or stream them to your phone or tablet.

TV shows

Cartoons are moving pictures. Children and grown-ups love them. They can be short shows or complete movies. They're usually funny.

A lot of people enjoy watching **sports** on TV. Some of the most popular sports in the world are soccer, basketball, tennis, and golf. What sports are popular in your country?

We watch the **weather** to find out if it's sunny, rainy, windy, or cloudy. What's the weather like today?

A **quiz show** is a kind of competition. One person asks others a lot of different questions. The winner is the person with the most points.

A **documentary** is a show that gives us information about our world. It can be about animals, history, or geography.

The **news** is about things that are happening in the world. It's on TV at the same time every day.

A **comedy** is a funny show that makes us laugh. What's your favorite comedy?

We watch a **series** in parts. These parts are called **episodes**. You can sometimes watch an episode every day.

 2 **Read again and answer.**

1 Which show can tell us things about animals?
2 Which show can be short or a complete movie?
3 Which show is about things that are happening in the world?
4 Which sport is one of the most popular in the world?
5 Which show can tell us to take an umbrella with us?
6 Which show is in episodes?
7 Which show is a kind of competition?
8 Which shows are funny?

 3 **Ask and answer.**

1 What's your favorite TV show?

> My favorite TV show is the news.

2 What's it about?

> It's about the news around the world.

3 Why do you like it?

> I like learning about what's happening in the world.

10 **Listen and say the show.**

 1 Goal! Sports.

cartoon   comedy   documentary   news
quiz show   rock music video   ~~sports~~   weather

2 **Choose the words to talk about the different shows.**

amazing   bad   boring   exciting   funny   good   interesting

I think quiz shows are more
interesting than the weather.

I think rock music
videos are the best.

3 **11–12** **Listen and complete the clocks. Listen and check. Do karaoke.**

I don't like TV, I don't like it much,
But there are some shows that
I sometimes watch.
On channel one at ,

There's a really good documentary
About animals and where they live,
What they do, and what they eat.
And on channel four at ⊘ ,

They put on a great cartoon.
At one o'clock and then at ⊘ ,

They show the news and then the weather.
They're not my thing, they're not for me,
But I like the sports at ⊘ .

But what I like, what I love the best,
Are the action movies, more than the rest.
They're on at ⊘

And at , but I want more.

4 **Read and complete.**

arrived   ~~four~~   news   thirty
turned on   waited

Tim and Jen went to the park last Saturday. They ran on the grass, played with a ball, and went on the swings. At ten to (1) _____four_____ they sat down because they were tired. They saw a newspaper on the bench. They opened it to the TV page and looked to see what was on the different channels. Tim wanted to go home and watch *Friendly* at four (2) _____. They went to the bus stop and (3) _____. The bus didn't come until quarter after four. They (4) _____ home at twenty-five to five, ran into the living room and (5) _____ the TV. The show wasn't *Friendly*, it was the (6) _____. They looked at the newspaper again. It was an old one! They showed *Friendly* on Friday, not on Saturday.

Sounds and life skills
Deciding together

1 Watch the video. What is the problem and what do they do about it?

Pronunciation focus

2 🎧 13 **Listen and underline the sounds *sh* and *ch*.**

EVA: Hi, Dad. Can we please change the channel? We want to watch *Top Talent*.

MR. SHARMA: Oh, I'm sorry, Eva. Not now. The golf's on – and you know I love golf!

SALLY: What time does it finish, Mr. Sharma?

MR. SHARMA: Oh, don't worry. It finishes at twenty to seven!

3 **Think and complete. Practice with a partner.**

A: Can we please change the channel and watch _____?

B: No, I'm sorry. I'm watching _____.

A: What time does it finish?

B: It finishes at _____.

4 **Look at the TV guide. Which two shows would you like to watch and why?**

5 In a group, discuss the TV shows and decide what to watch together.

Channel 1

17:00 Sing Up!
In this evening's semi-final contest, four singers sing their best songs with famous musicians. Vote to see your favorite in next week's finale!

18:30 Movie: Starshine
Dr. Dark has a plan to take away starlight from the universe. Can five young scientists and one spaceship stop him?

TV DOC 3

18:00 Shark Show
In this documentary, Shark Dave shows us one of the fastest fish on the planet: the shortfin mako.

18:30 Insect Investigation: Explore the world of magical dragonflies!

19:00 The Curious Chef
Shona travels to China to discover new lunch dishes to cook at home.

SPORT4U Live

17:10 Soccer-Crazy
Live: Sporting Galaxy vs. Chester City

18:30 American Basketball Special
Live: New York vs. Orlando

Useful language

Can/Can't we watch ...?
What time is it on?

Sounds and life skills: consonant clusters *sh* and *ch* | collaboration

Diggory Bones

1 **What can the thief do with the Baloney Stone program?**
What does Brutus Grabbe want?

How can we make nature documentaries

1 🎧 **15** **Listen and read. Which show doesn't show real animals?**

FILMING NATURE

There are some great nature documentaries coming out this month, so we wanted to hear from some of the people behind the magic. They told us about how new technology brings viewers closer to nature.

I started working as an underwater **camera operator** 30 years ago. Making documentaries was very different then. My video camera was big and heavy, with **batteries** that didn't last long. Unfortunately, there isn't much light **underwater**, so the cameras didn't film very well. Now, the technology is amazing! We use small low-light cameras and long-life batteries, so we can stay underwater for longer.

For *Discover the Deep*, I went deeper into the ocean than ever before. I filmed some incredible underwater animals we never knew about!

Adrian Hems, Camera Operator

New technology means we can now make really exciting nature documentaries. In *Migrations*, we used **drone cameras** to film animals **from the air**. We filmed hundreds of animals moving across the land together. In the past, we filmed from a helicopter. Some people still do that, but I think using drones is much better. You can get closer to the animals. In the first **episode**, I filmed the amazing elephant migration in Botswana.

Lucy Hall, Director of Photography

Working on *How Dinosaurs Lived* was so much fun! I create **computer animations** of animals and make them look real. Dinosaurs are **extinct**, so we filmed the landscape they once lived in. I created the dinosaurs with computer-generated images (CGI), and we added them to the landscape. The **effects** are excellent – much better than the ones I used for movies in the past. I created some amazing dinosaur fights!

Ben Sharp, Special Effects Technician

2 **Read again and complete the diagram.**

Past — big, heavy cameras

Present — small, low-light cameras

3 **Which show sounds more interesting to make and why?**

I'd like to watch *Discover the Deep*. Filming deep underwater sounds amazing!

Creating dinosaurs with special effects must be a lot of fun, so I really want to watch *How Dinosaurs Lived!*

— **FIND OUT MORE** —
What is the most expensive nature documentary ever made?

Read the chat message. Why did Quinn think the show was interesting?

12:00   % ▮

← 👤 **Fahad is online**   🔍 🏠 ☰

Quinn

Hi, Fahad. How are you?

Yesterday, I watched an amazing documentary called *City Animals*. It's about animals that live in big cities. You can watch it on the *Wildlife Channel* every Sunday.

Last night's episode was about foxes in cities. I found it really interesting because there's a fox that comes into our garden. Look at the picture that I took of it. Isn't it cute?

Some people are frightened of foxes, but they're shy animals. In the documentary, they explained that foxes now live among humans in towns because we are destroying their natural habitat.

You have to watch it because you can learn about some really awesome animals. Next week's episode is about owls. The photography is incredible, too!

 Underline the adjectives in the chat message in Activity 1.

  In pairs, discuss a nature documentary you know. Write your ideas in your notebook.

[What's the name of the documentary?]

[What's it about? Why is it interesting?]

Learning to write:

Adjectives

We use adjectives to describe things.

My video camera was big and heavy.

I created some amazing dinosaur fights!

Ready to write: ➡

Go to Workbook page 16.

Project

Make a presentation about a nature documentary.

2 People at work

 1 ▶ **Why does everyone have to leave the school? Watch and check.**

 2 ▶ **Watch again. Complete the sentences.**

1 They're looking around a _____ fair.
2 Robert thinks he's going to be a _____ .
3 Sally thinks she's going to be a _____ .
4 Sally hopes the _____ isn't going to burn down.
5 Eva's going to be a _____ .
6 They're going to write about _____ .

STUDY

I'm **going to be** a vet.
Eva **isn't going to be** a nurse.
What **are** we **going to write** about?

 3 **Read and order the words.**

1 write about / What / for our blog post? / are / we / going to
2 going to / a nurse / be / when I grow up. / I'm
3 a doctor. / going to / Eva / be / isn't
4 The school / isn't / burn down. / going to
5 win / prize! / We're / that / going to
6 do / you / What / tomorrow? / are / going to

 4 **Ask and answer.**

1 What are Sally, Robert, and Eva going to be? Do you think they will be good at those jobs?
2 What do you think you and your friends are going to be? Why?

18   **Language:** plans, intentions, and predictions with *going to*

1 ▶ Can you remember the last lesson? Watch the language video.

2 🎧 ▶ 16–17 Listen and order. Listen again and check. Do karaoke.

a She's going to help them all
And work in schools … ☐

b They're going to do their best,
Then sleep and play. ☐

c They're going to do the job,
Then work all day,
Then sleep and play … ☐

d She's going to show the kids.
She's going to teach good rules. ☐

f He's going to do his best,
Then sleep and play … ☐

e They're going to do the job,
They're going to work all day. ☐

g He's going to do the job.
He's going to work all day. [1]

3 Look and say. What are they going to do?

4 Correct the sentences.

a She's going to wash her face.
b They're going to go to a music festival.
c They're going to turn on a computer.
d She's going to play tennis.
e They're going to watch TV.
f He's going to wake up.

> a No, she isn't going to wash her face. She's going to brush her teeth.

5 📝 Write two more questions. Then ask your partner.

1 Where are you going to go after school?
2 Who are you going to see this evening?
3 When are you going to do your homework?
4 What time are you going to go to bed tonight?

6 📝 What are you going to do after school? Write 20–30 words.

Read the blog. Which three jobs did George Orwell have?

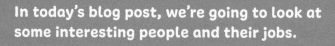

ALL BLOGS   MY BLOG   NEW POST

Kid's Box Reports

In today's blog post, we're going to look at some interesting people and their jobs.

Interesting jobs

Formula 1 is a car-racing competition. It's a team sport. One of the most important people on the team is the **mechanic**. Steve Matchett was a Formula 1 mechanic. He had to repair cars during the race. Now Steve works as a **sports commentator** on TV.

George Orwell was an important **writer**. Two of his most famous novels are *Animal Farm* and *1984*. He was also a **reporter** and wrote for different newspapers. Before he started writing, he was a **police officer**.

Alexia Putellas is a Spanish **soccer player** and is one of the best in the world. She has won awards for her skills, including UEFA Women's Player of the Year Award, the Ballon d'Or Féminin, and The Best FIFA Women's Player.

José Andrés is a famous **cook** who was born in Spain. He founded **World Central Kitchen**, which makes healthy food for people in countries going through difficult times.

Angelina Jolie is a famous **actor**. Her movies include *Maleficent* and the *Kung Fu Panda* movies. She also works to help people around the world. She loves planes, so she became a **pilot**, and she still enjoys flying now.

Shigeru Miyamoto designed the video games *Donkey Kong* and *Super Mario Bros*. When he was young, he studied art and wanted to be an **artist**, but then he discovered *Space Invaders* and decided to become a **video game designer**.

 Read again and answer.

1 Who is one of the most important people on a Formula 1 team?
2 What did Steve Matchett repair?
3 What are two of George Orwell's most famous novels?
4 What was George Orwell's job before he was a writer?
5 What did the soccer player win?
6 What did the cook do?
7 Who is a pilot and actor?
8 Which famous video games did Shigeru Miyamoto design?
9 Which two people help people in different countries?
10 How many of these people are on TV?

 Ask and answer.

1 Which job is the most exciting? Why?

> I think game designer is the most exciting job because you can design games that you like to play!

2 Which job would you like to have? Why?

> I'd like to be a cook so that I can taste delicious food all day!

1 🎧 18 **Listen and match. Say the job.**

🎧 **1** Good evening. This is Captain Bird speaking. Welcome aboard flight 241 from Dublin to London.

Pilot. That's e.

 **a**

 **b**

 **c**

 **d**

 **e** 1

 **f**

2 🎧 19 **Listen again and choose the right words.**

1 The plane is flying to **New York** / **London** / **Paris**.
2 The artist is painting **badly** / **quickly** / **carefully**.
3 The cook is making a **chocolate cake** / **carrot cake** / **cheesecake**.
4 Mr. Hamilton can get his car at **ten o'clock** / **half past nine** / **half past ten**.
5 The designer is **happy** / **tired** / **hungry**.
6 The reporter is going to interview a **soccer player** / **swimmer** / **basketball player**.

3 **Play the game.**
You get ten attempts.

Do you work at the fire station?

No, I don't.

Do you wear a uniform?

Yes, I do.

4 **Read and think. Ask and answer.**

What's William going to be when he grows up?

He's going to be a designer.

William	enjoys drawing and making things. He uses his computer to help him.
Teresa	likes writing and taking pictures for her blog.
Katy	loves playing with cars and repairing things.
Richard	loves making cakes and working in the kitchen.
Robert	loves acting. He's in the drama club at school.
Helen	loves drawing and painting.

5 **Think about someone you know who has an interesting job. Answer the questions.**

1 Who does this job?
2 What's his/her job?
3 What does he/she do at work?
4 Why do you think it's interesting?

6 📝 **Write about an interesting job. Write 20–30 words.**

Sounds and life skills
Thinking about the future

 1 ▶ **Watch the video. What jobs would they like to have when they grow up?**

Pronunciation focus

 2 🎧 20 **Listen and underline the jobs. Which job ends with the /ər/ sound?**

ROBERT: Look at this … a nurse. That's an interesting job! I think I'm going to be a nurse when I grow up.

SALLY: Hmm, a nurse? That's great, Robert. I think I'm going to be a dentist.

ROBERT: A dentist? I thought that you always wanted to be a doctor?

SALLY: Maybe I can be a doctor and a dentist!

 3 🎧 21 **Listen and complete. Practice with a partner.**

A: What _____ you going _____ be?

B: I think _____ going _____ be a _____ .

A: That's an interesting job!

4 **Look at the job ads. What kind of person do you need to be for these jobs?**

Chefs wanted!

We are looking for chefs for two new restaurants in Rome.

You have to be creative and speak Italian.

You have to be good at making interesting pizzas and working very hard.

Email: Bella@Pizzaperfect.it

URGENT! Are you a ski instructor? Come and work at Winter Wonderland Ski Center.

You have to love snow and mountains! You have to be patient and good at talking to people.

You have to be good at skiing and snowboarding.

Email: sam.cold@WWSC.co.gp

Useful language

A chef has to be creative.
A ski instructor has to be good at talking to people.

 5 **In a group, discuss different jobs and what you need for them.**

Diggory Bones

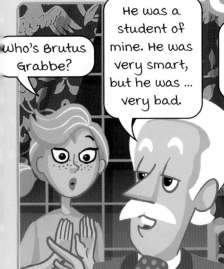

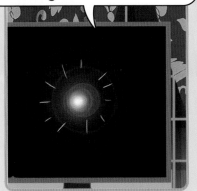

 1 **At what time is Diggory going to meet Brutus tomorrow? Why wasn't Brutus at the library?**

1 🎧 **23** **Listen and read. Why is it important to control fire?**

How can we use fire?

People learned how to make fire about a million years ago, and fire can be very useful. We use it for cooking and for heat when we're cold. It also gives us light.

What causes fire?

Did you know fire needs three things: oxygen, fuel, and heat? Oxygen is a gas that is in the air all around us. Some examples of fuel are wood, coal, paper, natural gas, and oil. When fuel gets very hot and mixes with oxygen, it can **start a fire**.

Not all fires are **man-made**, and a fire can start **naturally**, like in a forest. It can also start **by accident**, for example, when cooking at home. It's important to control fire because it can **spread** quickly and it's very dangerous when it gets **out of control**.

OXYGEN HEAT FIRE FUEL

How can we stop a fire?

Taking away the oxygen, fuel, or heat means a fire can't burn anymore. Water can **put out** a fire, but be careful: water can also start a fire if it has contact with electricity. So, never use water to put out a fire close to electrical equipment. Always use a **fire blanket** to cover the flames instead. It stops the oxygen and puts out the fire. Using **fire extinguishers** that spray foam is another way to stop the oxygen. A fire stops burning if there is no more fuel, so they sometimes **go out** on their own.

2 **Read again and choose the correct options.**

1 Fire burns with _____ and _____ .
   a fuel   **b** heat   **c** foam

2 Fires can start _____ or _____ .
   a by accident   **b** without fuel   **c** naturally

3 We use fire for _____ and _____ .
   a oxygen   **b** cooking   **c** heat

4 We can stop a fire with _____ or _____ .
   a water   **b** fuel   **c** a fire extinguisher

5 Fire is _____ and _____ .
   a easy to control   **b** quick to spread   **c** very hot

3 **How do you use fire safely in your daily life?**

In the backyard, we have a BBQ that my parents use in the summer.

We have a fireplace with a metal grate in front for heating the living room in the winter.

FIND OUT MORE
What are the main causes of house fires?

1 Read the safety brochure. How many dos and don'ts are there?

DID YOU KNOW…?
Firefighters have to get dressed in two minutes! The uniform is very heavy and made of special material to protect them from the heat.

2

Fire safety

- ✗ Never play with matches, candles, or other things that can start a fire.

- ✗ Don't put a lot of plugs in electric outlets.

- ✓ It's important to have smoke alarms in your house.

- ✗ Never play near stoves, fireplaces, or other areas where there is fire.

- ✓ Make sure you know the emergency phone number to report a fire.

- ✗ Never open any doors if there is fire on the other side.

- ✓ Go to a window and open it. Climb out if it's safe, or wait for help if you are upstairs.

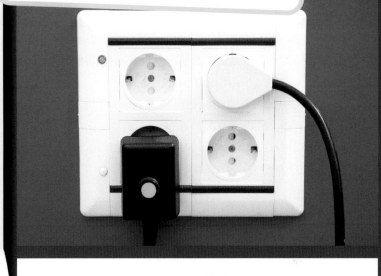

Always remember the number to call in an emergency!

2 Underline the imperatives with *always* and *never* in the safety brochure in Activity 1.

3 In pairs, discuss where safety advice is important. Write your ideas in your notebook.

Learning to write:
Imperatives with *always* and *never*
We use imperatives with *always* and *never* to show it is very important to do something.
Never use water to put out a fire close to electrical equipment.
Always use a fire blanket to cover the flames.

Ready to write:
Go to Workbook page 24.

Project
Make a poster about forest fire safety.

1 **Sarah is talking to her mother, Mrs. Smith. Read the conversation and choose the best answer. You do not need to use all the letters.**

a   Can we go to the park?

b   Yes, please. Can I call Katy to see if she can come?

c   My favorite comedy's on at twenty-five after five.

d   I think it's about half past eleven.

e   All right, then. Can I call Peter?

f   Thanks, Mom. Can you pass me the phone?

g   Which ones should I wear? My running shoes?

h   Does Peter like history?

Example

> **Mrs. Smith:** What time is it, Sarah?   **Sarah:** d

Questions

1   **Mrs. Smith:** What do you want to do?
    Sarah: _____

2   **Mrs. Smith:** OK. Put your shoes on.
    Sarah: _____

3   **Mrs. Smith:** Yes, the blue ones. Listen, do you want to go with a friend?
    Sarah: _____

4   **Mrs. Smith:** I think Katy's studying for a test this afternoon.
    Sarah: _____

5   **Mrs. Smith:** OK. Call him and see if he wants to come, too.
    Sarah: _____
    Mrs. Smith: Here you are. Tell Peter to bring his bike!

 2 **Tell your partner the story.**   > It's morning. The boy is going to school.

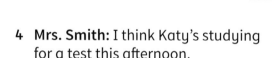

 3 📝 **Now write the story. Write 20–30 words.**

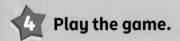

4 Play the game.

What are you going to do tomorrow?

Instructions: Go around the board. Say the time and what you are going to do at that time. Think of a different activity for each time.
To keep playing, you have to remember the activity that goes with each time. If you cannot remember, then go back to START and wait for another turn.

3 City life

Which places do you go to in your town or city?

1 ▷ **Why are they going in the wrong direction? Watch and check.**

2 ▷ **Watch again. Choose the right words.**

1 They arrive at **ten after two / twenty to three**.
2 They want information for their **blog post / school homework**.
3 They decide to visit a **bridge / museum** first.

4 They start outside a **store / school**.
5 They're lost because of problems with the **map / bus**.
6 Tower Bridge is **behind / across** the street.

3 **Read and complete the sentences.**

1 We have to go ⟶ this street.
2 We don't go across the river. We turn ↰ here.
3 Now we're at a ↰.
4 We have to take the third street on the ↱, and we walk □↑ this park.
5 Let's go ↖↑↗.
6 It's right ⇈ the street.

4 **Ask and answer.**

1 Why do you think Eva's dad said "no phones"?
2 Do you know how to read a map? Are you good at following directions?

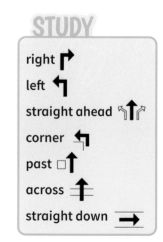

STUDY

right	↱
left	↰
straight ahead	↖↑↗
corner	↰
past	□↑
across	⇈
straight down	⟶

Can you remember the last lesson? Watch the language video.

 Look at the map. Read the directions and answer.

1   Go straight down Main Street. Take the third street on the left and go across the river. What's on the right?

2   Go straight down Main Street and turn right on Blue Street. Turn left on Low Road and then go across Green Street. What's on the corner, on the left, across from the music store?

3   Go straight down Main Street and take the second street on the left. Walk past the playground. What's next to it?

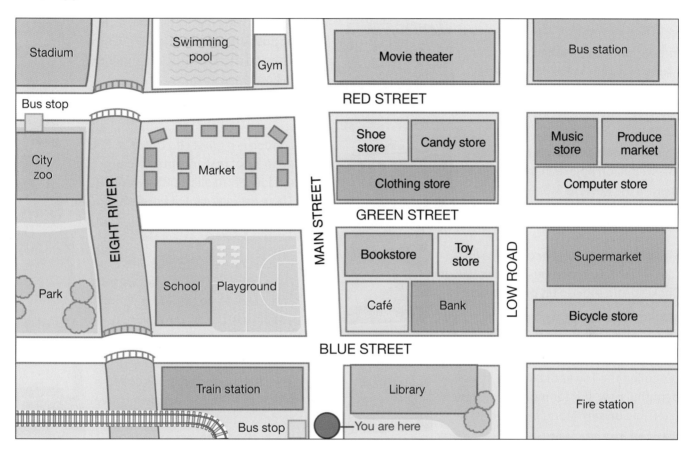

 🎧 24 **Listen to the directions and answer.**

> 🎧 1 Go straight ahead. Take the second street on the left. What's at the end of the street?

 Play the game.

> The river.

> Go straight down Main Street and take the third street on the right. Go across Low Road, and it's next to the music store.

> Is it the produce market?   Yes, it is!

 Write the directions to (1) the bank and (2) the gym.

1 **Read the blog. Which airport is the busiest in the U.K.?**

ALL BLOGS | MY BLOG | NEW POST

Kid's Box Reports

London is the capital city of England and the U.K. Yesterday we went there and saw a lot of interesting places. Here are some of our pictures.

London

New Scotland Yard is one of the most famous **police stations** in the world. A king of Scotland lived in the first Scotland Yard.

This is the British **Museum**. There are six million objects here. One of them is the Rosetta Stone.

This is the new Globe **Theater**. The first Globe Theater was famous because William Shakespeare showed his plays there.

This **castle** is next to Tower **Bridge**. It's called the Tower of London. It looks beautiful now, but for many years it was a terrible **prison**. Many people died here.

You can mail letters or postcards at **post offices** or at a red mailbox. They painted the first red mailbox in London in 1874.

London is a great city to eat in. There are a lot of **restaurants**, and you can eat food from all over the world. There are also a lot of **hotels** to stay in.

London has six airports. This is Heathrow. It is the busiest **airport** in the U.K. More than 70 million people use this airport every year!

This is a London **taxi**. It's called a black cab. Black-cab drivers have to pass a test to show that they know all the **streets** in London.

2 **Read again and correct the sentences.**

1 A king of England lived in the first Scotland Yard.
2 You can see the Rosetta Stone at the Natural History Museum.
3 Shakespeare showed his movies at the Globe Theater.
4 They painted the first London mailbox red in 1974.
5 London is a difficult city to eat in.
6 London has seven airports.
7 The Tower of London was a post office for many years.
8 London buses are called black cabs.

3 **Ask and answer.**

1 Do you think London is an exciting city? Why?

> I think London is an exciting city because there's a lot to see and do.

2 Where in London would you like to go? Why?

> I'd like to go the Globe Theater to see a play.

1 🎧 ▶ 25–26 **Listen and complete. Listen and check. Do karaoke.**

3

| bridge | castle | ~~museum~~ | park | restaurant | station | street | taxi | theater | zoo |

Theater, movies,
Restaurant, and hotel,
Museum, castle,
A story to tell.

I went to London
To have a nice day.
To go to a (1) _museum_ and
The (2) _____ for a play.

I saw Tower (3) _____
And the (4) _____, too,
Walked in the (5) _____,
And went to the (6) _____.

I went to a (7) _____
On the corner of the (8) _____.
I sat outside, and
I had something to eat.

I took a (9) _____
Because it was late.
My train was in the (10) _____.
It was half past eight.

2 **Ask and answer.**

| actor | bus driver | ~~cook~~ | doctor | firefighter | pilot | police officer | teacher |

Who works in a restaurant or hotel?   A cook.

3 **Look at the map. Ask and answer.**

Where's the museum?   It's between the gym and the library.

4 **Think of a place you know. Give directions for how to get there from your school. Can your partner guess?**

Go out the door, turn left, take the second street on your right, and walk past Flower's Restaurant. What can you see?   Is it the stadium?   Yes, it is.

Sounds and life skills
Choosing options

1 ▶ Watch the video. Where are the young people and how do they feel?

Pronunciation focus

2 🎧 27 **Listen. What do the circled words have in common?**

SALLY: OK! Let's look at the map! How do we get there?

ROBERT: We're (standing) outside the train (station).

SALLY: So, we have to go (straight) down this (street).
We don't go across the river. We turn left here at the (sporting) goods (store). Let's go!

3 🎧 28 **Listen and complete. Say the words. Can you think of more?**

s t r eet, _____ aight

_____ and, _____ adium, _____ udy

_____ orts, _____ anish

4 In pairs, discuss the best places to visit in your town/city and why you like them. Complete the table.

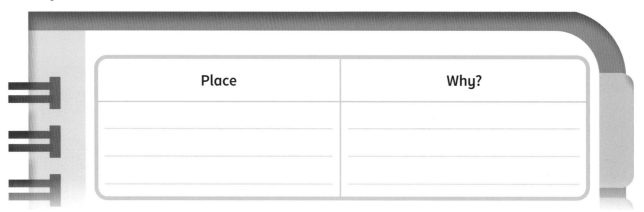

Place	Why?

5 In a group, choose one place to take a visitor to in your town/city.

Place _____

Where is it? _____

How can you get there? _____

What can you do there? _____

Useful language

Where should we go?
... is the most famous.
How do we get there?

Diggory Bones

③

 1 **Where was the most important library in the ancient world?**
Who was the taxi driver?

What are the best modes of transportation?

1 🎧 30 **Listen and read. What do the different types of transportation have in common?**

Want to hang out on the world's oldest elevated railway?

Then you have to ride on Wuppertal's hanging train! It's a train where the cars "hang" under the **tracks**. Every year, more than 25 million passengers travel on this **public transportation system**, which opened in 1901. It's the easiest way to see this German city because you don't get **stuck in traffic**. It's electric, too, so it's more **environmentally friendly** than cars or buses.

Travel in the sky!

The city of Medellín in Colombia is built on many hills, so it's not the easiest place to get around. That's why they built the **cable car** system in 2004. Now it's the most popular form of public transportation in the city! It's a fun way to travel, and you get great city views. It doesn't cause **air or noise pollution**, so it's **greener** than buses and taxis.

Are you in a hurry?

The Shinkansen in Japan is the fastest **high-speed** rail system in the world. It uses the **newest technology** to give thousands of passengers a fast and comfortable ride every day. The Shinkansen's electric trains use less energy, so they cause less pollution than cars and planes. That's a great reason to use the country's high-speed **rail network**!

2 **Read again and complete the table.**

	Germany	Colombia	Japan
Type of transportation	hanging train		
Advantage for passengers	You don't get stuck in traffic.		
How is it environmentally friendly?	It's electric.		

3 **Which mode of transportation is your favorite and why? How do you like to travel around?**

> I think the best way to travel is in a cable car because there are great views.

> I like to travel around on trains because they're quicker than buses.

FIND OUT MORE

What are the most environmentally-friendly modes of transportation in your country?

Geography: city life | critical thinking

1 Read the ad. What are the advantages of using an e-scooter or e-bike?

3

Public transportation is getting greener

Public transportation in our city is changing!

If you don't have a car and the buses or underground trains are overcrowded, why don't you use two wheels instead? Our e-scooters and e-bikes are the newest and easiest modes of transportation in the city. Just download our app and get moving! You can travel on the streets or in bicycle lanes at a speed of up to 25 km/h. Our e-scooters and e-bikes are quicker than walking, which means they're the best choice when you're in a hurry.

They're healthier than cars and buses because they don't cause air pollution. That has to make them the greenest transportation option in the city! Don't forget your helmet!

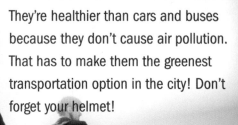

2 Underline the superlatives and circle the comparatives in the ad in Activity 1.

3 In pairs, discuss modes of transportation where you live. Write your ideas in your notebook.

Learning to write:

Comparatives and superlatives

We use comparatives to talk about two things.

They're **healthier than** cars and buses.

We use superlatives to talk about one thing from a group of the same things.

That has to make them **the greenest** transportation option in the city!

Project

Design a new, "unusual" mode of transportation.

Ready to write:

Go to Workbook page 34.

What kind of weather do you like or dislike?

4 Disaster!

1 ▷ Why did the boat catch fire? Watch and check.

2 ▷ Watch again. Order.

1 At first, the phone didn't work! But then he tried again.
2 Why didn't you go back to the beach?
3 Now we have a new idea for our blog – disasters!
4 We couldn't leave the island, so Dad had to call for help!
5 Dad was listening to the radio. They said a storm was coming!
6 We weren't taking pictures – we were running away.

☐
☐
☐
☐
1
☐

STUDY

Were you **listening** to the weather on the radio?

We **weren't listening** to the radio.

We **were listening** to music.

3 Read and match.

1 They were getting warm
2 The sky went dark
3 Robert wasn't feeling well,
4 When they were walking up the beach,
5 They didn't get a picture of the fire

a lightning hit the boat.
b because they were running away.
c when the reporter arrived.
d when they were sailing to the island.
e so they were taking care of him.

4 Ask and answer.

1 How do you think each of the three children felt during the disaster?
2 How do you think they feel now? Why?

1 **Can you remember the last lesson? Watch the language video.**

2 🎧 ▶ **31–32** **Read and guess. Listen and check. Do karaoke.**

climbing   eating   playing   sailing   sitting   skating   swimming   ~~walking~~

What were you doing when the storm began,
When the lightning hit and the water ran?
Where were you when the rain came down,
On the mountain, at the beach, in the forest, or the town?

I was (1) __walking__ up the mountain.
He was (2) _____ over the lake.
We were (3) _____ in the park.
She was (4) _____ a piece of cake.
They were (5) _____ in the river.
He was (6) _____ on the ocean.
She was (7) _____ up a wall.
I was (8) _____ under a tree.

3 **What were you doing when it happened? Write three sentences.**

(hurt my knee) (dropped my cell phone) (lightning hit the tree) (started to feel sick)

(teacher saw me) (cut my hand) (it started to rain) (my mom took a picture of me)

4 **Play the game. You get five attempts.**

I was having a picnic when it started to rain.

(What was I doing when it started to rain?) (Were you having a picnic?) (Yes, I was.)

5 **Choose one of your sentences and continue the story. Write 20–30 words.**

1 What did you do?   **2** What happened next?

Read the blog. How high was the wall of seawater in Messina?

ALL BLOGS   MY BLOG   NEW POST

Kid's Box Reports

Disasters sometimes happen, as we recently found out. We decided to find out about some famous disasters.

Disasters

This ship is named the *Titanic*. On April 14, 1912, it was sailing across the Atlantic Ocean when it hit an **iceberg**. They couldn't see the iceberg because of the fog.

The Hindenburg was one of the biggest airships ever built. On May 6, 1937, when it was arriving in the U.S.A., it caught fire. People think it happened because **lightning** hit it during a **storm**.

Hurricanes are very dangerous storms with strong winds. The worst Atlantic **hurricane** in history was the Great Hurricane in 1780, on October 10–16.

When a **volcano** erupts, it throws hot liquid rock and gases into the air through the hole at the top. When Krakatoa erupted on August 26, 1883, it made the loudest sound ever heard.

On November 1, 1755, an earthquake hit Lisbon, Portugal. The ground moved for ten minutes. The **earthquake** destroyed most of the buildings in the city.

On December 28, 1908, a **tsunami** hit Messina, Italy. The enormous wall of seawater was about ten meters high. How high do you think the seawater is in this picture?

 Read again and correct the sentences.

1 The *Titanic* hit an iceberg on July 14, 1912.
2 The *Titanic* was sailing across the Pacific Ocean.
3 The Hindenburg disaster was on May 16, 1937.
4 The Hindenburg airship was arriving in the U.K.

5 The Great Hurricane was in 1870.
6 Krakatoa, the volcano, erupted on August 28.
7 The Lisbon earthquake was on November 1, 1575.
8 The tsunami was on October 28, 1908.

 Ask and answer.

1 Which disaster do you think was the worst? Why?

2 What was the worst weather you can remember? What were you doing?

> I think the earthquake was the worst disaster because the ground moved for ten minutes.

> I remember a hurricane. I was playing with my brother at home.

1 🎧 33 Listen and repeat the chant.

January, February, March,
April, May, June,
July, August, September,
October, November, December.

2 🎧 34 Listen and say the months.

🎧 **1** It's sunny and windy. There are a lot of red apples on the trees …

September.

January

February

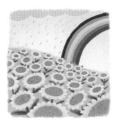
March

April

May

June

July

August

September

October

November

December

3 Ask and answer.

It's February.

What can you see?

Some children are reading comic books. They're sitting in their living room next to the fire.

4 Cross out the extra word.

1 What were they to doing on Wednesday, November 13?
2 There was a very bad storm on the May 31.
3 They couldn't see because of was the fog.
4 Why was do he running?
5 The lightning hit many my car on August 19.
6 My birthday was in the January.
7 The fire did started on June 29.
8 In Antarctica, there's a the lot of ice.

5 📝 Read the notes and write about what happened.

Friday, March 13, was a terrible day for Jane. What happened?
when / go downstairs / put / foot / on / toy car
fall down / break / leg
ambulance / come / take / to the hospital
when / nurses / carry / Jane / into the hospital / drop
now / Jane / in the hospital / with / broken leg / and / broken arm

When Jane was going downstairs, she put her foot on a toy car.

Sounds and life skills
Thinking creatively

1 Watch the video. When did the young people feel afraid, excited, sick, and worried?

Pronunciation focus

2 🎧 **35** **Listen and write the circled words in the correct sound column in the table.**

REPORTER: Why didn't (you) go back to the (beach)?

SALLY: Because (we) were (close) to the (island).
So we decided to (wait) there for the weather to get better.

ROBERT: Yeah, we were walking up the beach to find somewhere (safe) when (lightning) hit the (boat) and it caught fire!

SALLY: We couldn't leave the island, so Dad had to call for help!

A	E	I	O	U
sailing	me	sky	hello	rescue

3 🎧 **36** **Listen and complete the rhyme with the words from Activity 2.**

There's a bad storm with rain and _____.
The _____'s on fire, and it's very, very frightening.
The helicopter is _____, we all can see.
It's coming to _____ my friends and me!

4 Look at the quiz in the magazine and write two more questions.

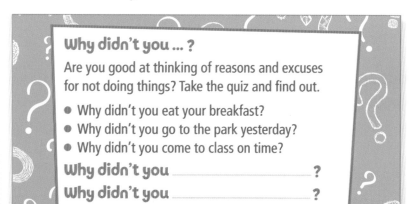

Why didn't you ...?

Are you good at thinking of reasons and excuses for not doing things? Take the quiz and find out.

- Why didn't you eat your breakfast?
- Why didn't you go to the park yesterday?
- Why didn't you come to class on time?

Why didn't you _____?
Why didn't you _____?

5 In pairs, ask and answer questions from the quiz. Can you think of interesting reasons?

Useful language
Why didn't you ...?
Because ...

Sounds and life skills: the vowel sounds | 🛡 creative thinking

Diggory Bones

Give me the Baloney Stone! You ... you ...

You can have the stone back when you help me get what I want.

That group of stars is called the Canis major, which means "the big dog."

And the brightest star on the dog's nose is called Sirius.

What's the date today, Emily?

WHIISS

July 21, why?

Today is the beginning of the Ancient Egyptian year.

WHISS

There's the cave over there!

Night's falling, and a storm's coming. It's going to be very dark!

Is it too dangerous for you, Bones?

No, I understand these places better than you, Brutus. I'm not afraid.

WHISS

In the Ancient Egyptian calendar, Sirius showed the opening of the New Year.

Today it's going to show us the "opening" of the secret cave!

It's really hot down here.

When we were looking at the stars, I remembered the terrible disaster.

A volcanic eruption destroyed ancient Alexandria, and then a tsunami covered the city with water.

PLOP BUBBLE BUBBLE

BOOM

Aagh! We're walking near a volcano!

CRACK

BOOOM

Run to the light, Emily!

Aagh!

⭐ **What terrible disaster happened in ancient Alexandria?**
Why is it going to be very dark?

Story: unit language in context

Where can we find volcanoes?

1 🎧 **38** **Listen and read. What causes volcanoes?**

www.planetwonderswow.com

Pacific Ring of Fire

Have you ever heard of Pompeii? On August 24, in the year 79, nearly 2,000 years ago, a nearby volcano called Vesuvius erupted and covered the city of Pompeii in rock and **ash**.

Vesuvius is in Italy, but did you know that there are volcanoes all over the world and that one of the most active zones is the Pacific Ring of Fire? It's an area in the Pacific Ocean where there are almost 75% of Earth's volcanoes.

There are so many volcanoes around the Ring of Fire because of **tectonic plates**, which are layers of rock just below **Earth's crust**. The places where two plates meet are called **plate boundaries**, and when the plates move, which they do a lot, mountains and volcanoes form between them. Many of these plates meet at the Ring of Fire, which is why so many volcanoes appear in the area.

The movement of tectonic plates also causes earthquakes, and around 90% of them happen along the Pacific Ring of Fire.

One of the positive things that comes from the Pacific Ring of Fire is **geothermal energy**. **Magma** is the name of the very hot liquid rock that is deep underground. Around the Pacific Ring of Fire, magma is very close to the Earth's crust, which makes it easier for engineers to use this heat from the ground as a **source of green energy**.

They can use this energy to heat houses, make hot water, and even make electricity. Many countries, including the United States, Indonesia, Japan, New Zealand, and the Philippines, already use geothermal energy.

2 **Read again and complete the diagram.**

> tectonic plates   magma
> Earth's crust   plate boundary

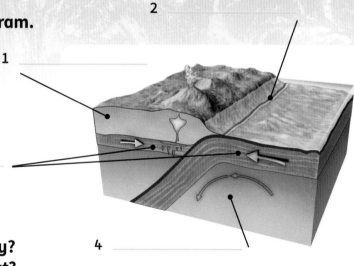

1 _____

2 _____

3 _____

4 _____

3 **Are there volcanoes in your country? Are they active, dormant, or extinct? What other volcanoes do you know about?**

> There are a lot of volcanoes in my country, but they're all dormant.

> I know about Mount St. Helens, which is an active volcano in the United States.

FIND OUT MORE
What is the largest volcanic eruption in history?

Geography and history: natural landscapes | 🛡 critical thinking

1 Read the email. What is Iceland famous for?

To: Petra   **Subject:** Iceland is amazing!

Hi Petra,

During summer vacation, I visited the amazing island of Iceland, which is a volcanic island in the North Atlantic Ocean. It is famous for its dramatic geography.

In Iceland, you can see geysers, which are holes in the ground that blast out jets of water and steam. There are also natural hot springs, huge lava fields, and glaciers. In fact, glaciers cover 10% of the island. Sometimes there are volcanic eruptions, and I learned that, back in 2010, a volcano erupted and filled the sky with ash. It meant that planes in about 20 countries couldn't take off!

Iceland uses its interesting geography to make electricity. In fact, the island makes electricity by using power from its rivers and waterfalls and heat from the ground, which is very good for the environment.

I hope I can go back to Iceland again one day because it is a fantastic place. I'll tell you more about my trip when I see you!

Bye for now,

Eric

2 Underline *which* to give extra information in the email in Activity 1.

Learning to write:

Which to give extra information

We can use *which* to give extra information.

There are so many volcanoes around the Ring of Fire because of tectonic plates, **which** are layers of rock just below the Earth's crust.

3 In pairs, discuss places you know that are famous for their landscape. Write your ideas in your notebook.

Ready to write:

Go to Workbook page 42.

Project

Make a presentation on a volcanic eruption.

1 Read the letter and write the missing words.

Dear Aunt Anika,

I'm writing to tell you about the great time we had last weekend.

I think Mom told you we were going to Manchester on Saturday.

Well, we went to the ___stadium___ to see a soccer game because

Manchester United was playing against Liverpool. I really enjoyed

it, but, sadly, Liverpool didn't (1)_____.

They (2)_____ 1–0.

On Sunday, we spent the day exploring the city.

We got lost because we didn't have a (3)_____.

No problem! We asked a police officer for (4)_____, and he showed us where to go.

We visited the Lowry Museum, which had some interesting paintings by a famous

(5)_____ from Manchester, L.S. Lowry. There are pictures of the museum and the

stadium attached to this email. Hope you like them.

Love,

Jamie

2 🎧 39 Listen and write. There is one example.

1 Who was he visiting: _____grandpa_____

2 Where did they go first: _____

3 Address: _____ Road

4 Opening times: From 10:00 to _____

5 Where they had lunch: _____

6 Transportation home: _____

3 Play the game.

Find your way home

Instructions: Go around the board following the instructions. When you stop on a picture, spell the word. If it's right, roll again. If it's wrong, stop.

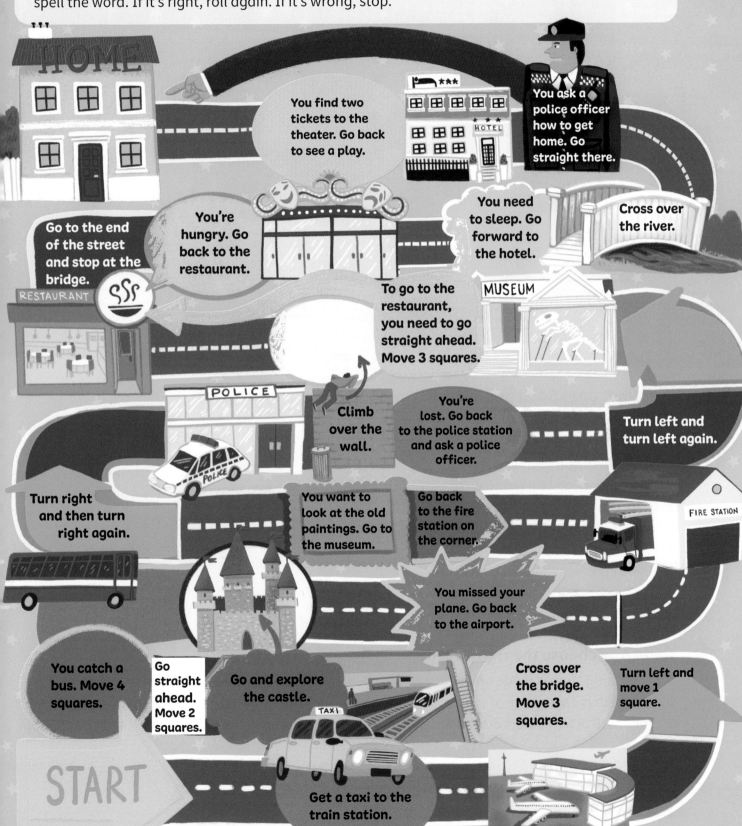

You find two tickets to the theater. Go back to see a play.

You ask a police officer how to get home. Go straight there.

Go to the end of the street and stop at the bridge.

You're hungry. Go back to the restaurant.

You need to sleep. Go forward to the hotel.

Cross over the river.

To go to the restaurant, you need to go straight ahead. Move 3 squares.

Climb over the wall.

You're lost. Go back to the police station and ask a police officer.

Turn left and turn left again.

Turn right and then turn right again.

You want to look at the old paintings. Go to the museum.

Go back to the fire station on the corner.

You missed your plane. Go back to the airport.

You catch a bus. Move 4 squares.

Go straight ahead. Move 2 squares.

Go and explore the castle.

Cross over the bridge. Move 3 squares.

Turn left and move 1 square.

START

Get a taxi to the train station.

5 material things

What can you find in a joke store?

1 ▶ **What does Sally put her teeth in? Watch and check.**

2 ▶ **Watch again. Say "yes" or "no."**

1 The candy store is made of brick. *Yes.*
2 The children go to a pet store.
3 The eggs are made of fur.
4 Robert wants to buy some toys.
5 The teeth are made of sugar.
6 The snakes are made of paper.
7 The spiders are made of rubber.
8 Sally's afraid of spiders.

STUDY

The eggs **are made of** white chocolate.
The spider **isn't made of** fur.
What **are** they **made of**?

3 **Read and choose the right words.**

1 The candy store is made **on / of** brick.
2 The teeth **is / are** made of sugar.
3 The small black spiders are **made / make** of fur.
4 The eggs **is / are** made of white chocolate.
5 The snake is made of **rubber / stone**.
6 The spider on Sally's shoulder **is / isn't** real.

4 **Ask and answer.**

1 What did you think of Eva and Robert's joke with the spider?
2 Look around your classroom. What are things made of?

Language: describing objects

Can you remember the last lesson? Watch the language video.

 Ask and answer.

> **a** What's the school made of?   I think it's made of stone.

   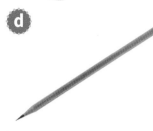

  Listen and check.

> 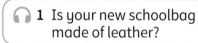 **1** Is your new schoolbag made of leather?   Yes, it is.   That's c.

 Read and match.

1 This is my favorite hat. I can wear it every day because it changes with the weather. When it's raining, it has two pieces of plastic to cover my ears. [c]

2 When it's cold, a special scarf, which is made of fur, comes out to cover my neck. [ ]

3 When it's sunny, my hat protects me from the sun. I also have sunglasses made of special plastic to protect my eyes. [ ]

4 These are my favorite shoes. I wear them on the weekend. They are purple. [ ]

5 I don't need to wear socks with my new shoes. They keep me cool in the summer. They're blue. Look! [ ]

6 If I jump or drop the shoes on the floor, they bounce. The shoes can help me jump very high – up to two meters! That is because they are made of a special rubber called "bounce-a-lot." I'm going to bounce to the park. Goodbye. [ ]

 Read again and correct the sentences.

1 The hat changes every day.

2 When it's raining, it has two pieces of plastic to cover his eyes.

3 The sunglasses are made of special rocks.

4 The shoes can help her swim.

5 If you drop the shoes, they dance.

6 The shoes are made of wood.

1 Read the blog. What's the most important material? Why?

ALL BLOGS · MY BLOG · NEW POST

Kid's Box Reports

Materials can be man-made or natural. We make man-made materials in factories. We get natural materials from rocks in the ground, animals, or plants. Here are some interesting things made of different materials.

Materials

Most houses are made of **bricks**, **stone**, or **wood**, but Édouard Arsenault used 12,000 **glass** bottles to build this amazing house.

Cardboard and **paper** come from trees. Cardboard is stronger than paper. This tower is made of thin **cardboard**, and the bridge is made of paper.

Gold and silver are precious metals. This car is made of 80 kilograms of gold and 15 kilograms of **silver**. The tires aren't made of **metal**, but you have to drive it very carefully!

SHAMPOO

Most animals have **fur**, but sheep have **wool**. We use wool to make fabric for clothes. We can also make things at home from wool. Look at these beautiful cushions. The covers are made of wool.

A lot of things are made of **plastic**. Today we use plastic more than any other material in the world. We have to recycle plastic. When we recycle something, we use it again in a different form. This bottle of shampoo is made of recycled plastic.

2 Read again and answer.

1. Where do we make man-made materials?
2. What are most houses made of?
3. How many glass bottles did Arsenault use to build his house?
4. How much gold is in the car?
5. Where do cardboard and paper come from?
6. Where does wool come from?
7. What are the cushion covers made of?
8. What does "recycle" mean?

 3 Choose five materials. Tell your partner about things made of these materials.

My book is made of paper and cardboard.

1 Read and choose the right words.

1 Paper and cardboard are made of **wood** / **leather** / **metal**.
2 Gold comes from **animals** / **the ground** / **trees**.
3 Wood comes from **the ground** / **trees** / **flowers**.
4 Fur comes from **trees** / **sand** / **animals**.
5 Glass is made of **leaves** / **sand** / **wood**.
6 Wool comes from a **sheep** / **cow** / **bear**.

2 41–42 Listen and order. Listen and check. Do karaoke.

a This table's made of wood,
And that skirt's made of grass. ☐

f This box is made of silver.
That watch is made of gold. ☐

b From rocks, plants, or animals,
Or from a factory. ☐

g Everything's material,
Everything we see, ☐ 1

c This scarf is made of wool,
And I wear it when it's cold. ☐

h Books are made of paper.
Their covers are made of cardboard. ☐

d This chair is made of metal.
That bowl is made of glass. ☐

e Some things are made of plastic,
Which can be strong and hard. ☐

3 Close your book. What can you remember from the song?

What's the bowl made of?

It's made of glass.

4 Look around your classroom. Find and write two things for each material.

wood	metal	glass	plastic	paper
pencil				

5 What are things made of in your classroom? Write 20–30 words.

Sounds and life skills
Talking about different ideas

 1 ▷ **Watch the video. Which stores do they go in?**

Pronunciation focus

 2 🎧 43 **Read and listen. What happens to the last sound in the first word in blue?**

EVA: Ooh – look at this candy store! It's fantastic!
SALLY: Yeah, and it's all made of brick.
ROBERT: Come on, let's go inside!
SALLY: In a minute!

3 🎧 44 **Listen and complete. Practice with a partner.**

1 Come _____ .
2 Look _____ !
3 Look _____ this.
4 You're _____ star.
5 I have _____ great idea.
6 _____ a minute.

 4 🎧 45 **Look at the game. Listen to the young people playing it and mark (✓) the phrases they use.**

The yes/no game

a stuffed toy car

a toy car

a skateboard

a bicycle

a tablet

a drawing pad

a magnifying glass

a cup

Is it big? ☐
Is it long? ☐
Is it made of wood? ☐
Is it made of paper? ☐
Is it made of metal? ☐
Does it have legs? ☐
Does it have pages? ☐
Do you use it to play? ☐
Do you use it to learn? ☐

Wait a minute. ☐   You're a star! ☐   Come on. ☐
Nice one! ☐   Look at this. ☐

Useful language

Is it made of …?
Does it have …?
Do you use it to …?

 5 **In pairs, play the game.**

Diggory Bones

 Where was Brutus carrying the Baloney Stone? Which two materials are the different bowls made of?

Story: unit language in context 51

What can you make with recycled materials?

1 🎧 **47** **Listen and read. What materials do they use?**

Giant Faucet, Switzerland

I saw this amazing **sculpture** in a park in Winterthur. It looks like a faucet is **magically** hanging in the air, but it's actually a simple **illusion**. Water from underground travels up a pipe, which holds the giant metal faucet in place. We can't see it because the water flows over it when it comes out.

Everyone stops to look at it **carefully** to see how it works. It feels magical, and that's the idea of art – to create something different that surprises us.

The Bruges Whale, Belgium

This giant whale is made of **plastic waste** from the Pacific Ocean, and when you look **closely**, you can see that there are thousands of **plastic objects**, from trash cans to toilet seats! Two **artists** created the sculpture to show how much we're polluting our world. Did you know there's more plastic in our oceans than whales!

A lot of artists are working with **recycled materials** now, which is important because it connects art with the world around us. I love how creative and interesting this sculpture is.

Puppy, Spain

This huge dog sculpture sits outside a museum in Bilbao. It's very special because it's **completely** covered in plants – about 38,000 flowers in total! Metal pipes **inside** a **hidden** frame send water to the plants to keep them alive.

I love that the **sculptor** uses nature because it shows that art is always growing and changing. The artist wanted to create something to make people happy, and I think this sculpture really does that.

2 **Read again and complete the table.**

	Giant Faucet	The Bruges Whale	Puppy
What is it made of?	metal, (1) _____water_____	recycled (4) _____	metal (7) _____, (8) _____
How was it made?	Water travels up a (2) _____ and flows out of the faucet.	The artists collected plastic (5) _____ from the Pacific Ocean.	Water travels through pipes to keep the (9) _____ alive.
What is the message?	It shows that art can (3) _____ us.	It gives the message that we're (6) _____ our world.	Art is (10) _____ and (11) _____.

3 **How do the sculptures make you feel and why? What other sculptures do you know about?**

> This sculpture makes me laugh.

> I saw a metal sculpture of a bear and a tree in downtown Madrid.

FIND OUT MORE
What is the biggest sculpture in the world?

5

1 **Read the review. What message does the artist want to give?**

Domestic towers

I saw some amazing sculptures in Germany last week. They are "Domestic towers," and I liked them because they are actually three sculptures in one.

There are three towers painted brightly, and each one is skillfully made with household objects.

The green tower is made of recycled objects you find in gardens, and there's a pot at the center with a flower growing in it. The blue tower is made of tools, paint cans, and other things you might find in your garage.

The red tower is my favorite because each time I look at it, I see something new.

There are tires, boxes, sports equipment, a keyboard, and a video camera. There's even a bike at the top!

I love the way the artist skilfully linked all the objects together. It shows how creative we can be because these beautiful things are made of everyday objects or trash.

2 **Underline the adverbs in the review in Activity 1.**

3 **In pairs, discuss a sculpture or statue that you like. Compare the materials used in each one. Write your ideas in your notebook.**

Sculpture	Materials

Learning to write:

Adverbs

We use adverbs to describe how we do something.

It looks like a faucet is **magically** hanging in the air.

It's **completely** covered in plants.

Ready to write:

Go to Workbook page 52.

Project

Make or draw a sculpture out of recycled materials.

6 Senses

1 ▶ **What do they want to make for their next blog post? Watch and check.**

2 ▶ **Watch again. Order.**

1 It smells like Robert's socks.
2 What does it feel like?
3 I like pineapple on my pizza.
4 It sounds like someone's falling down the stairs.
5 What does this taste like, Robert?
6 In this week's science club, we're going to look at the five senses.
7 What does this smell like, Sally?
8 It's very soft. It feels like fur.

> **STUDY**
>
> What does it **look / feel / taste / smell / sound like?**
> It **looks / feels / tastes / smells / sounds like** coffee.

(order boxes; box 6 marked **1**)

3 **Read and order the words.**

1 a / truck. / sounds / My / car / like

_____

2 feels / like / His / jacket / fur.

_____

3 does / taste / What / like? / that / soup

_____

4 our / mother / look / Who / like? / does

_____

4 **Ask and answer.**

1 How did the kids explore their senses? Which one was your favorite?

2 Talk about your family. Who do you look like?

54   **Language:** describing sensations

Can you remember the last lesson? Watch the language video.

2 🎧 48 **Listen. What does it sound like?** 1. It sounds like a car.

3 **Play the game. What does it sound like?**

- Think of five things that make different sounds.
- Write the words on five small pieces of paper.
- Give your pieces of paper to your teacher.

- Play the game with the class.
- Make the sounds and guess.
- Now play the game in groups.

Tick tock tick tock.   It sounds like a clock.

 Ask and answer. What does it look like?

What do you think number 1 looks like?   I think it looks like a cat's nose.   So do I.

 Ask and answer. What does it feel like?

What does number 1 feel like?   It feels soft and furry.

1 **Read the blog. What ingredients would you put on your pizza?**

ALL BLOGS   MY BLOG   NEW POST

Kid's Box Reports

We wanted to learn how to make pizza, so we went to Luigi's Italian Restaurant and spoke to Mario, the cook. Before we started, we washed our hands.

Making pizza

First we made the base. The base is made of **dough**. We put some flour, **yeast**, salt, and water into a **bowl** and **mixed** them well. Then we let the dough sit for an hour so it could grow.

Then we put tomatoes, cheese, salami, olives, and onion on top of the base. After that we added some black pepper and cooked it in the **oven** for 15 minutes.

When it was ready, we put the pizza onto a **plate**. Mario uses special plates in the restaurant. They're very big, and they're made of wood.

You can eat pizza with your hands, but you need to **cut** it with a **knife** first. This one is round, but pizzas can also be square.

We had the pizza with salad. We used a big **spoon** and **fork** to mix it. Here's a picture of our delicious meal. It looks good, but it tasted even better!

2 **Read again and correct the sentences.**

1 Before they started, they washed their feet.
2 Pizza base is made of rubber.
3 They put some flour, yeast, salt, and milk into a bowl.
4 They put some black chocolate on top of the pizza.
5 They cooked the pizza in the oven for 25 minutes.
6 The plates are very big, and they're made of glass.
7 Mario used a spoon to cut the pizza.
8 They mixed the salad with a knife and fork.

3 **Talk about your favorite meal. Tell your partner which ingredients you need.**

My favorite meal is pasta with meat sauce. I need pasta, water, tomatoes, meat, and onions.

1  49–50 **Read and match. Listen and check. Do karaoke.**

My name's Mario.
I'm an Italian cook.
If you want to make a pizza,
Then listen to me and look. `e`

Take salt, yeast, flour, and water,
Put them in a bowl.
Mix them all together,
And wait for it to grow. ☐

When the base is bigger,
Throw it in the air.
Use your hands to turn it,
Don't get it in your hair. ☐

Now you choose your topping:
Tomato, pepper, and cheese.
You can choose anything:
Sausage, onion, and meat. ☐

Cook for 15 minutes,
Then put it on a plate.
Cut it with a knife and fork,
Mmm. Now that tastes great! ☐

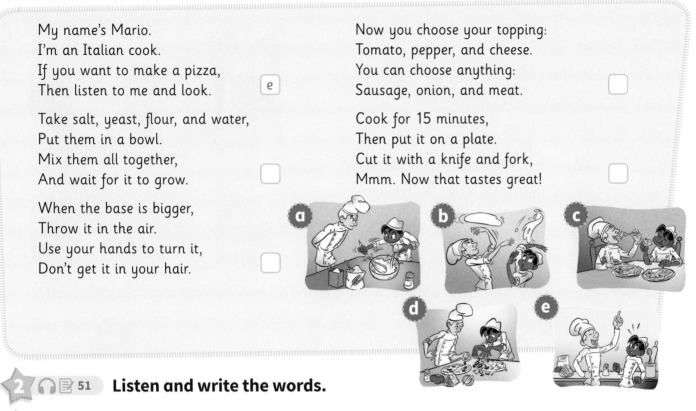

2 51 **Listen and write the words.**

3 **Read and complete. Write the recipe in your notebook.**

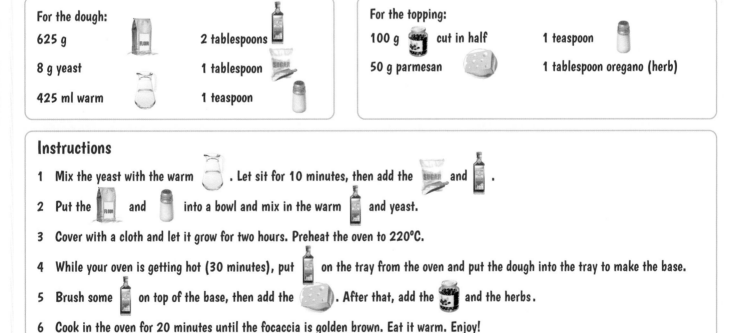

Ingredients

For the dough:
625 g
8 g yeast
425 ml warm
2 tablespoons
1 tablespoon
1 teaspoon

For the topping:
100 g   cut in half
50 g parmesan
1 teaspoon
1 tablespoon oregano (herb)

Instructions

1   Mix the yeast with the warm   . Let sit for 10 minutes, then add the   and   .

2   Put the   and   into a bowl and mix in the warm   and yeast.

3   Cover with a cloth and let it grow for two hours. Preheat the oven to 220°C.

4   While your oven is getting hot (30 minutes), put   on the tray from the oven and put the dough into the tray to make the base.

5   Brush some   on top of the base, then add the   . After that, add the   and the herbs.

6   Cook in the oven for 20 minutes until the focaccia is golden brown. Eat it warm. Enjoy!

4 **Think about your favorite meal. Write a shopping list of the ingredients.**

Sounds and life skills
Describing sensations

⭐**1** ▶ Watch the video. What do they touch, hear, smell, and taste?

Touch

Pronunciation focus

⭐**2** 🎧 52 Listen and underline the stressed words.

EVA: Put your hand in the box. What does it feel like?

SALLY: It's very soft. It feels like fur. Is it an animal?

ROBERT: No, it's my toy spider.

⭐**3** 🎧 53 Listen and underline the stressed words. How is the meaning different?

1 This is my toy spider.

3 This is my toy spider.

2 This is my toy spider.

4 This is my toy spider.

⭐**4** 🎧 54 Complete the poem with the words in the box. Listen and check.

birds ~~light~~ shower toast toothpaste

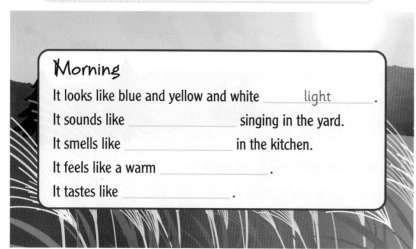

Morning
It looks like blue and yellow and white _____light_____ .
It sounds like _____ singing in the yard.
It smells like _____ in the kitchen.
It feels like a warm _____ .
It tastes like _____ .

⭐**5** 📝 In pairs, write a poem about a season, time of year, time of day, or a favorite place. Describe what it feels like.

Useful language
What does it ... like?
It ... like ...

Diggory Bones

1 **What's a "snake bowl"? What does Diggory use to get Brutus out?**

How do we make noises?

THE SCIENCE OF SOUND

Sounds are created when objects **vibrate**. And these **vibrations** are called **sound waves**. We can't see them, but they travel through the air until they reach our ears, and we hear them as sounds.

If we shake a tiny bell, it vibrates quickly, so we hear a high ring in our ears. If we hit a large bell, the sound waves are stronger and vibrate more slowly, so we hear a low sound.

Some sounds can be high but very loud. Did you know that a baby's cry is louder than the honk of a car horn? However, the loudest sound on Earth is low and loud – it's the sound of a volcano erupting!

Sound needs to travel through something, like an object or air or water. If there is no air, like in space, there is no sound! Wind is air, but it has no sound. It's the wind blowing against an object that makes the sound.

Sound travels four times faster through water than air, so it can travel farther through water. That's how whales can hear each other even when they are hundreds of kilometers apart!

2 **Read again and choose the right words.**

1 Vibrations that create sound are called sound _____. **a** energy **b** waves
2 Fast vibrations make a _____ sound. **a** high **b** low
3 Slow vibrations make a _____ sound. **a** low **b** high
4 Sound needs to travel through something, like _____ or water. **a** air **b** space
5 Wind makes sound when it blows against _____. **a** objects **b** air
6 In water, sound travels _____ than in air. **a** faster **b** slower

3 **Close your eyes and listen. What can you hear? What sounds do you like and dislike?**

I can hear traffic outside the school. I don't like it because it's too noisy.

I can hear myself breathing. I like it because it relaxes me.

FIND OUT MORE
What is the maximum speed of sound?

1 **57** **Read and listen to the poem. Which sound doesn't the writer like?**

Sounds I love to hear

I love to hear my cat meowing because it means she wants me to cuddle her.

I love to hear the "ding-dong" of the doorbell ringing because it means we have a visitor.

I love to hear my friends giggling because it means they are happy and having fun.

I love to hear plates clattering in the kitchen because it means dinner will be ready soon.

I love to hear rain tapping on my window because it makes me feel cozy and safe inside.

But I hate to hear cars zooming outside because it makes me feel stressed.

2 **Underline the sound words in the poem in Activity 1.**

Learning to write:

Sound words

We use sound words to help the reader hear the sounds we are writing about.

If we shake a tiny bell, we hear a high **ring**.

A baby's cry is louder than the **honk** of a car horn.

3 **In pairs, brainstorm sounds that you love and sounds that you hate. Explain why. Complete the table in your notebook.**

Sounds I love	Sounds I hate

Ready to write:

Go to Workbook page 60.

Project

Make a poster about your favorite sounds.

Review Units 5 and 6

1   **Read the text. Choose the right words from the table and write them on the lines.**

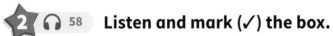

Wall | Find friends | Chat | Profile

Hi everyone,
Here are a few lines to tell you about (1) _____ our _____ soccer team. We're (2) _____ the Cambridge Flyers. We (3) _____ indoor soccer on weekends, and we play against other teams from towns near ours. There (4) _____ seven of us on the team. We always change players (5) _____ only five can play at a time. (6) _____ week we played against the team from Oldcastle. They played really (7) _____ , and they won 4–1.
We (8) _____ the first goal, but then they scored the next four. We're going to win our next game though.
That's all for now,
Li Wei

1	(our)	we	us
2	called	calling	call
3	plays	playing	play
4	is	am	are
5	but	because	so
6	Next	Every	Last
7	well	good	beautiful
8	marked	scored	do

2 🎧 58   **Listen and mark (✓) the box.**

1   When is David's birthday?

A ✓   B ☐   C ☐

2   What is he going to do on Saturday?

A ☐   B ☐   C ☐

3   What time is the party?

A ☐   B ☐   C ☐

4   Where are they going to go?

A ☐   B ☐   C ☐

5   What was his favorite present last year?

A ☐   B ☐   C ☐

6   What would he like to get this year?

A ☐   B ☐   C ☐

3 Play the game.

Collect the materials

Instructions: The winner is the first person to get seven things made of different materials. Roll the dice and move your counter. Say what you can see and what it's made of. If you're right, take another turn. If you're wrong, stop.
If you stop on something made of a material that you already have, you lose a turn.

FINISH

START

7 Natural world

What kinds of nature problems do you know about?

 1 Why are they picking up trash? Watch and check.

 2 Watch again. Say "yes" or "no."

1 They have five days to write their next blog post. *No.*
2 Sally thinks they should put some sunblock on.
3 A woman's taking glass bottles and plastic bags out of the lake.
4 She has to do this every day.
5 People should look for a recycling bin.
6 The kids shouldn't tell their friends about the problem.

STUDY

People **should take** their trash with them.
They **shouldn't leave** it on the grass.
What **should** we **do** about this?

 3 Read and match.

1 It's very sunny,
2 When the sun is strong,
3 We shouldn't leave
4 We should always
5 We shouldn't throw our
6 What should we

a do to help?
b our trash on the grass.
c trash into lakes or rivers.
d clean up after a picnic in the country.
e so we should put our hats on.
f we should use sunblock.

 4 Ask and answer.

1 Why was the woman cleaning up the lake?
2 What do you do with your trash when you're outside?

Language: giving advice

1 ▶ **Can you remember the last lesson? Watch the language video.**

 2 **Read the posts and choose the right words. Who do you agree with? Why?**

 How can we help look after our world?

Plastic isn't good for the planet. We **(1) should / shouldn't** stop using plastic. It can take 1,000 years to disappear, and we are filling the whole Earth with ugly, terrible, dirty plastic. It's a disaster! We really **(2) should / shouldn't** buy plastic bags or plastic bottles.

Oliver, 13

There is water all around us – in fact more than 70% of the Earth is water. We **(3) should / shouldn't** decide how to use water as carefully as we can so that in the future we have water to drink, cook, and wash our clothes. Everyone **(4) should / shouldn't** remember to turn off faucets and take short showers instead of baths.

Pablo, 11

We use energy for everything, from video games to playing the electric guitar, but making it causes pollution. So, you **(5) should / shouldn't** remember to turn everything off when you finish playing and save energy.

Maria, 12

Did you know that every year we throw away more than a billion tons of food? That's frightening! You **(6) should / shouldn't** try to prepare only the food that you need. If you have any food left, you can share it with your friends.

Li Jing, 12

3 **Read the questions and write the name.**

1 Who thinks that we can save food and be kind to others? _____
2 Who thinks that we need a plan for the future? _____
3 Who thinks that something we use takes a long time to disappear? _____
4 Who thinks that we need to do something very important after we have fun? _____

 4 🎧 ▶ **59–60** **Read and guess. Listen and check. Do karaoke.**

clean   climb   ~~drop~~   go   jump   put   run   stop   walk

You shouldn't ___drop___ your garbage,
You should _____ it in a garbage can.
You shouldn't leave it on the ground,
You should _____ up everything.
Here comes the bear, here comes the bear!
It's coming for your lunch!

Should I move, or should I _____ ?
Should I _____ that tree?
I should do something now.
That bear / cow is after me.

You shouldn't _____ across the field.
You should _____ around.
You shouldn't go too near that cow,
It can push you to the ground.
You should _____ ...
You should _____ quickly!

 5 📄 **How do you think we should take care of our world? Write 20–30 words.**

1 Read the blog. Which animal fact is the most interesting to you?

ALL BLOGS · MY BLOG · NEW POST

Kid's Box Reports

Nature watch

There are more than 15,000 endangered species of animals, and even more species of insects in danger, like butterflies. Let's take a look at what people are doing to protect them so that they do not become extinct.

There are two special National Parks in Siberia to protect Siberian tigers from people who want to catch them for their beautiful striped fur.

Tigers are an endangered species, and we should protect them. When we protect tigers, we protect forests, which give people around the world clean air, water, food, and materials.

Another animal famous for its stripes is the mountain zebra. Thanks to conservation projects, mountain zebras are now safe from extinction.

The Lost Ladybug Project asks people to take pictures of this beetle if they see it and post them online.

This is a nine-spotted lady beetle. It has four black spots on each wing and one in the middle of its body. It lives in North America, and it is an endangered species.

Did you know that the last day of April every year is Save the Frogs Day? There are educational events in more than 56 countries.

Frogs are in danger all over the world. The frog in the picture is a Lehmann's poison frog. It is found in Colombia. It has red, orange, or yellow stripes.

Let's celebrate beautiful butterflies! Every two years there's a Butterfly Beauty Festival in Asia from November to March. It helps us to protect butterflies and learn more about them.

Butterflies are beautiful, flying insects. This butterfly is a purple spotted swallowtail. It has white spots on its purple wings. Every year millions of butterflies fly to a different place to escape cold weather. That can be dangerous, but we can help by protecting their habitats.

2 Read again and answer.

1 How many endangered species are there?
2 How do the special parks in Siberia protect the tigers?
3 When we protect tigers, what else do we protect?
4 Which animal has a spotted body and wings?
5 Where does the Lehmann's poison frog live?
6 Which animal has red, orange, or yellow stripes?
7 When is the Butterfly Beauty Festival?
8 Which animal has white spots on its wings?

3 Ask and answer.

1 Which animal would you like to protect? Why?
2 What should we do to protect this animal? Think of a class project.

1 **Look at the pictures. Describe them to your partner.**

Queen Alexandra's birdwing butterfly

Male

Female

The female is brown.

The male is more beautiful than the female.

7

2 🎧 61 **Listen. Write words or numbers.**

MARY'S PROJECT 🦋

Name of butterfly	1	Queen Alexandra's birdwing
Wings measure (male)	2	cm
Wings measure (female)	3	cm
Description (female)	4	
Description (male)	5	

3 **Read and complete.**

butterflies   extinct   should   ~~thousands~~   trees   yard

Help endangered species

There are **(1)** _thousands_ of endangered species in the world. "Endangered" means there is time to help them before they disappear. They are not **(2)** _____. So, what should we do? We **(3)** _____ take care of our world and ask everyone to help make it a cleaner place for animals to live in. We should make oceans, ponds, streams, and the air much cleaner than they are now — and you can help, too!

You can:
- help clean and protect the habitat in your **(4)** _____, near your house, or at your school.
- plant **(5)** _____ and flowers where insects, like **(6)** _____, can live.
- help projects to plant riverbanks with plants that make the ground stronger and give animals a habitat.

4 **Look at the pictures. Talk about what you should do.**

I think we should recycle all bottles.

Yes, I agree.

 a
 b
 c
 d
 e
 f

Sounds and life skills
Taking care of your community

 Watch the video. Where are the young people and how do they feel?

Pronunciation focus

 62 **Listen and underline the stressed words.**

EVA: People shouldn't leave their trash on the grass or throw it in the lake.

ROBERT: So, what should they do with it?

PARK RANGER: They should look for a recycling bin or take their trash home with them.

 Think and write. Practice with a partner.

A: People shouldn't _____ .

B: What should they do?

A: They should _____ .

 Read the flyer. What information does it give?

 **COMMUNITY ACTION!**

Let's clean it up!
Here's how to organize your own neighborhood clean-up.

Get permission	Ask your family for permission to do a clean-up in your neighborhood. Ask an adult to help you.
Decide where	Where do you want to pick up trash? Is there a park or a beach close to you that needs to be cleaned?
Get help	Find friends and family to join the clean-up. The more people, the better! Ask local stores or your local government if they can give you free trash bags, gloves, or tools.
Take pictures	On the day of the clean-up, take a lot of pictures that you can share afterward.
Say "thank you"	Thank everyone for their help.

NOTES: OUR NEIGHBORHOOD CLEAN-UP

Where	
When	
Who should we ask for help?	
Who should take pictures?	

 In a group, plan your own neighborhood clean-up and make notes.

Useful language
Let's do … on …
What should/shouldn't we do?
We should/shouldn't …

That wasn't very smart, Brutus.

Run and get help, Dad!

I don't think you should leave your daughter down here with a snake, Bones.

With two snakes, Brutus! One has spots and stripes, but the other doesn't.

HISS

Now there's only one snake – an ugly, weak one!

Now, Bones, you should turn on the computer for the instructions to get out of here.

You need the instructions to get out of here, but I don't!

You should move slowly and carefully, Emily. This ladder's old, and it isn't very strong.

OK, Dad!

Wait for me!

The famous butterfly room of Queen Hetepheres! most people thought this was only a story.

There are thousands of butterflies!

They're all orange and black striped with white spots on their wings.

You shouldn't touch anything, Brutus.

Aagh! Striped insects!

They're the young butterflies! Here are their parents to protect them!

 1 **Why should they climb the ladder slowly and carefully? What do the butterflies look like?**

How can we help endangered species?

1 🎧 64 **Listen and read. Why are these animals endangered?**

Turtle

I joined the Turtle Protection Project two years ago. Turtles come to our beach each year to lay their eggs, but they are an **endangered species**. Humans are a big problem because they catch turtles to sell their eggs, meat, and shells.

The project teaches people why we should **protect** turtles, and now people in the community help take care of the beaches and keep the turtles safe.

Every year, we save thousands of turtle eggs from danger. Our project really makes a difference.

Veronica

Orangutan

I volunteer at an orangutan rescue center near my village. Orangutans are one of the most endangered animals in the world. Humans are destroying their **natural habitat** by cutting down the jungle for buildings, roads, and farming.

Our center helps orangutans that are in danger. We feed them and help the sick ones get better. It's like a school, too. We teach them how to **survive in the wild** so that when they're ready, the orangutans can go back to a safer part of the jungle.

Umar

Hummingbird

At school, I'm learning about the endangered species in my city, like the hummingbird. This little bird is in danger because the city is growing. There are more and more new buildings, so the hummingbird is losing its habitat.

I want to protect hummingbirds because I think we should help protect all endangered species. In my yard at home, we planted flowers and we hung some food and water feeders from the trees. The trees in the yard also **provide shelter** so that the birds have a safe place to build nests. I'm happy because now I see hummingbirds in our yard all the time.

Alejandro

2 **Read again and complete the table.**

	Turtles	Orangutans	Hummingbirds
Project	Turtle Protection Project	orangutan rescue center	school project
What is the problem?	People catch turtles to sell their eggs, meat, and shells.		
How are people helping?	They take care of the beaches and keep turtles safe.		

3 **Which of the projects would you like to help with? Why?**

I love hummingbirds, so I'd like to help with that project.

I'd like to help in the orangutan rescue center because orangutans are my favorite animals.

FIND OUT MORE
What are the biggest causes of animal endangerment?

Geography: endangered species and conservation | social responsibilities

1 Read the student report. How do bees help plants survive?

DID YOU KNOW...?
Bees are so noisy because they beat their wings about 230 times per second!

7

Protecting bees

Why are bees important?

Bees are so important because they help plants survive. When a bee eats the sugary nectar from inside a flower, its hairy legs pick up some pollen. Pollen is the yellow powder on flowers. When the bee goes to another plant, it rubs some of the pollen onto it and that pollinates the plant. Without bees, some plants might disappear.

Another reason why bees are important is that they make honey. Honey is food for the bees in winter, but humans and other animals enjoy it, too!

Why are bees endangered?

Bees are endangered because farmers use chemicals called pesticides on plants to kill the insects that eat them. Unfortunately, when farmers use these chemicals, they also kill bees.

How can we help?

- We should plant flowers that bees like in our yards or on our balconies, and of course, we shouldn't use pesticides.
- We should also buy local honey. When we do that, we help beekeepers in our area.
- Lastly, let's remember to talk about bees and why they are so important.

2 Underline the facts with *when* in the student report in Activity 1.

 3 **In pairs, discuss why it is important to protect endangered species and how you can help them. Complete the table in your notebook.**

Why is it important to protect endangered species?	How can we help?

Ready to write:

Go to Workbook page 70.

Learning to write:

Facts with *when*

We use *when* to give facts.

When humans cut down trees, we destroy orangutans' natural habitat.

When we provide shelter, we give them a safe place to build nests.

Project

Create a fact file about an endangered animal.

Geography: endangered species and conservation | learning to learn

8 World of sports

Which sports do you like?

 1 Who wins a prize for the first time? Watch and check.

 2 Watch again. Complete the sentences.

1 Today's the _____ prize day.
2 Good luck with the _____ .
3 He's _____ over the mats.
4 He hasn't climbed over the _____ .
5 He's lost the _____ .
6 He's stopped to help a _____ .

STUDY

We've **done** it.
He **hasn't lost**.
Have you ever **won** a prize?
  Yes, I have. / No, I haven't.

 3 Read and choose the right words.

1 **We're** / **We've** going to give the prize to the winners.
2 I've **ever** / **never** won any prizes!
3 He's **gone** / **go** back!
4 He's **walk** / **walked** along the bench.
5 He **haven't** / **hasn't** lost.
6 We've **doing** / **done** it!

 4 Ask and answer.

1 Do you think Robert did the right thing?
2 Which is more important: winning or helping your friends?

1 ▶ **Can you remember the last lesson? Watch the language video.**

2 **Use the words to talk about the pictures.** ~~begin~~ cook jump paint walk wash

> **1** They're going to begin the race. | They're beginning the race. | They've begun the race.

1 **a** **b**  **c**

2 **a** **b**  **c**

3 **a**  **b**  **c**

4 **a**  **b** **c**

5 **a**  **b** **c**

6 **a** **b**  **c**

3 🎧 65 **Listen and answer the questions.**

1 What has she done?
2 What have they done?
3 What has he done?
4 What has Michael done?
5 What have they done?
6 What has Robert done?

4 **Read and order the words.**

1 recently. / visited / He's / his / grandmother
2 you / Have / ever / basketball? / played
3 never / ice-skating / before. / been / She's
4 He / yet. / his / hasn't / done / homework
5 won / first / We've / prize!
6 entered / the / Have / they / competition?

Practice: present perfect   73

1 **Read the blog. What time of year do people do your favorite sport?**

ALL BLOGS   MY BLOG   NEW POST

Kid's Box Reports

When we do some sports, we need the right weather.

Sports for all seasons

Track and field is a sport that we usually do outside. It's difficult to do in the cold and rain, so, at school, we do it in the **summer**. A lot of people play **golf**. You can play golf in any season of the year, but not when it snows!

We can only do some sports in the **winter** because we need snow and ice. A lot of people enjoy **skiing** during winter vacation. Today a lot of young people like **snowboarding**, too. **Sledding** is also really fun in the winter. You can sled down a hill.

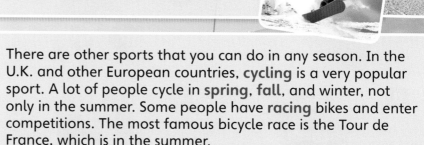

There are other sports that you can do in any season. In the U.K. and other European countries, **cycling** is a very popular sport. A lot of people cycle in **spring**, **fall**, and winter, not only in the summer. Some people have **racing** bikes and enter competitions. The most famous bicycle race is the Tour de France, which is in the summer.

The dates for the seasons are different in different parts of the world. In Europe, North America, and Asia, spring is from March to June, but in Australia, Africa, India, and South America, it is from about September to December.

2 **Read again and correct the sentences.**

1 At school, they do track and field in the fall.
2 It's easy to do track and field in the cold and rain.
3 You can play golf in the snow.
4 To do winter sports, we need fog and rain.
5 People go sledding in the summer.
6 Spring comes between autumn and winter.
7 Winter comes after summer.
8 The Tour de France is a snowboarding race.

3 **Ask and answer.**

1 Which sports do you enjoy doing in the summer? Why?
2 Can you practice any of these winter sports where you live? Why?

I enjoy playing basketball in the summer because I can play outside.

I can go sledding where I live because it snows in the winter.

1  **66** **Listen and write the words.**

2 🎧 ▶ **67–68** **Listen and order. Listen and check. Do karaoke.**

a Some like playing soccer.
Some like watching it. ☐

b We've skated in the park.
We've made a ball to throw. ☐

c We've played golf with Grandma.
We've raced against the clock. ☐

d We've skied down a mountain.
We've climbed up a rock. ☐

e We love sports, swimming, sailing, running!
We love sports.
We love to do it all. [1]

f It's good to move your body.
DON'T JUST SIT! ☐

g We've played badminton and tennis.
We've gone sledding in the snow. ☐

3 **Read and complete. Answer the questions.**

> hill ~~mountains~~ skiing sledding
> snowball snowboard snowboarding

This morning, Jane is coming home from her vacation in the (1) ____mountains____
with her family. She's had a great time. During the week, her mother and father
went (2) _____ every morning, but Jane and her older brother Frank
went (3) _____. After lunch, Jane and her brothers played in the snow.
They tried to play volleyball with a big (4) _____, but it was very
difficult because the snow was too soft. On the last day, they all went
(5) _____ together. Jane's parents and brothers kept falling and rolling
down the (6) _____, but Jane was very good at it. She wants to buy a
(7) _____ and go to the mountains again next year.

1 Where did Jane go on vacation?
2 Who did she go with?
3 What did her parents do every morning?
4 Which of Jane's brothers went sledding with her?
5 What did they try to play volleyball with?
6 What did they all do on the last day of their vacation?

Sounds and life skills
Working together

 1 ▶ **Watch the video. How does Robert feel? How does Robert's friend feel?**

Pronunciation focus

 2 🎧 69 **Listen and write the words in the correct form.**

SALLY: Yeah! He's _____ (jump) over the mats, and he's _____ (walk) along the bench, but he hasn't _____ (climb) over the wall. Come on, Robert! You're almost _____ (finish)!

 3 🎧 70 **Listen to the verbs. Complete the table.**

/t/ ending	/d/ ending	
		decided
		wanted
		needed
		waited

 4 **Robert is talking to his friend in the race. Read and match.**

1 Hey, are you alright?
2 Would you like some help?
3 OK. If you hold the rope, I can push you up.
4 There you go!

a Good idea!
b Yes, I think so.
c Thank you so much!
d Yes, please!

 5 **In a group, complete the teamwork challenge.**

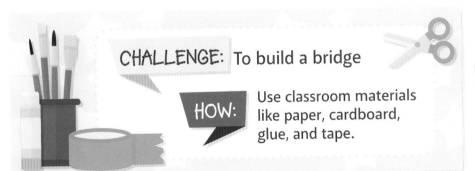

CHALLENGE: To build a bridge

HOW: Use classroom materials like paper, cardboard, glue, and tape.

Useful language
Would you like ...?
If you ..., I can ...
Let's ...

Sounds and life skills: endings /t/, /d/, and /id/ | 🛡 emotional development

Diggory Bones

1 **Which sports did the Ancient Egyptians invent? Where did Diggory send the email from?**

How do people train for different sports?

1 🎧 72 **Listen and read. Which sport should you do with a trainer?**

LET'S GET ACTIVE!

Sports and exercise are very healthy hobbies that people enjoy all over the world. There are so many different types to choose from, but did you know that there are two types of exercise? There's **aerobic** exercise, which means "with air," and **anaerobic** exercise, which means "without air." Let's find out more.

LONG-DISTANCE RUNNING

This is a great example of an aerobic sport. When you run, you need to **breathe** faster and deeper, so **oxygen** travels from your **lungs** to your **heart**. Then your heart sends oxygen around your body to your **muscles**. When you do aerobic exercise, you can breathe in enough oxygen to exercise for a long time. If you want to be a long-distance runner, train slowly in the beginning. Over time, you will build up your **endurance** and be able to run farther and longer. One day, you might run a marathon!

WEIGHTLIFTING

This is an example of an anaerobic sport. When you do an anaerobic exercise, you cannot breathe in enough oxygen to do the exercise for very long. Weightlifters do short, repeated, and very difficult exercises for about 90 seconds. That means they have to take a lot of breaks. Weightlifters use all the **muscle groups**, and their goal is to increase **strength**.

If you want to try weightlifting, it's important to ask a trainer for help. If you do an exercise incorrectly, it's easy to get hurt.

FIELD HOCKEY

Lastly, like most sports, field hockey is both aerobic and anaerobic. When a player runs across the field, they use aerobic energy, and when they hit the ball, they use anaerobic energy.

Think about other sports and the types of energy they use. Try a new sport today and comment below! Happy exercising!

2 **Read again and choose the correct word.**

1	It builds up endurance.	(aerobic) / anaerobic
2	It means "with oxygen."	aerobic / anaerobic
3	It means "without oxygen."	aerobic / anaerobic
4	It is a long exercise.	aerobic / anaerobic
5	It is a series of short exercises.	aerobic / anaerobic
6	It develops strength.	aerobic / anaerobic

3 **What sports do you like doing and why?**

I like playing soccer because it increases my endurance and I can play with my friends.

I exercise every day, and I really like gymnastics because it makes me stronger.

 **FIND OUT MORE**

What is the most popular sport in your country? Is it mostly aerobic or anaerobic?

Physical education: aerobic and anaerobic exercise | critical thinking

1 Read the brochure. Why is swimming a good hobby?

DID YOU KNOW...?

The fastest time recorded for an athlete to complete a marathon while running backward is 3:43:39.

Try swimming!

It's never too late to try swimming, and there are a lot of reasons why it's an amazing sport. Firstly, water is all around us, so it's important to know how to be safe in and near water.

Another reason why you should go swimming is that it is very, very healthy. Swimming is an intense aerobic workout. It uses a lot of different muscle groups, so it's a great way to get stronger and in better shape.

Finally, swimming is a great sport to do both alone and on a team. You can swim alone and take some time to think about your day, and you can make some new friends and enter competitions as a team. It's so much fun!

If you're a beginner, or maybe you haven't been swimming for a long time, get back in that pool and enjoy it. It's such a healthy hobby!

 2 Circle the words that help organize the writer's ideas in the brochure in Activity 1.

Learning to write:

Organizing ideas

We use *firstly*, *first of all*, *secondly*, *another reason is*, *lastly*, and *finally* to organize ideas.

First of all, soccer is a great team sport.

Lastly, like most sports, field hockey is both aerobic and anaerobic.

 3 In pairs, discuss other sports and why they are good for you. Write your ideas in your notebook.

Ready to write:

Go to Workbook page 78.

Project

Research a sport and make a poster to present to the class.

Review Units 7 and 8

1 **Look at the picture. Talk about it in pairs.**

It's a sunny day.

The little boy is playing with a red car.

Daisy

Sally

Vicky

Fred

John

Paul

Jack

2 🎧 73 **Listen and draw lines. There is one example.**

3 **Read the story. Choose the right words and write them on the lines.**

> are   can   clothes   dangerous   Have   ~~kicked~~
> quiet   sandwiches   shouldn't   water

I went to the beach with Sam and his dad last weekend.
We took a picnic and a ball. We were playing soccer on the
beach when I _____kicked_____ the ball into the ocean! It was
soon far out in the (1) _____!

"Can you swim?" Sam asked.

"No, I've never learned to swim!" I answered. "Can you swim?"

"Yes," said Sam, and he started swimming.

The waves were huge.

Sam's dad started shouting at him, (2) "_____ you
seen the flag? You shouldn't swim when there is a red flag!" Sam's dad swam toward him and pulled
him back to the beach.

"Sorry, Dad," Sam said. "The ocean was (3) _____!"

"Um. Should we have our picnic, now?" I asked.

We went to get our picnic, but it wasn't there.

"You (4) _____ leave food on the beach!" Sam's dad said. "The birds always eat it. Look!"

It was true. We saw a lot of big white birds eating our (5) _____.

Now choose the best name for the story. Mark (✓) one box.

A day at the beach ☐

The dangerous birds ☐

A nice swim ☐

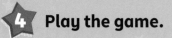

4 Play the game.

What's the question?

Instructions: Play in pairs. One player is **red** and the other is **blue**. Take turns going around the board. Read the answer and ask the question. **If your question is right**, score 3 points, **if it's wrong**, lose 1 point. Make a note of the points in your notebook.

17 It's Mr. Jones, the geography teacher.

18 I had lunch with my mom.

19 There are 365.

20 I've won two.

FINISH

16 I'd like the book on history, please.

15 It sounds like a dog.

14 Because I wanted to ask you about our homework.

13 I always go on the bus.

9 I always brush them three times a day.

10 We went to the park yesterday.

11 It tastes like cheese.

12 They're blue, green, and white striped.

8 There are five: two math books and three English books.

7 He's 71.

6 The eighth month is August.

5 It feels like hair, but it isn't.

START

1 I go to bed at half past nine.

2 They taste sour and delicious.

3 We should recycle them.

4 I had cereal and a glass of milk.

1   **Look at the picture. What's wrong? Talk to your friends.**

> Look at *a*. What do you think is wrong?

> She doesn't have her book for the class.

2 🎧 74   **Listen and check. Say the letter.**   🎧 1 He's worried because he's late.   That's *b*.

3   **Ask and answer.**

1   What should the children do to start their class on time?
2   Which of the things in the picture do you never do?
3   Which of the things in the picture do you sometimes do?
4   What should you do to be a better student?

1 **Read and answer the questions.**

1 How did Holly break her leg?
2 Why did she hit her head?
3 Who helped her?

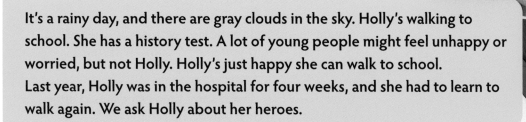

Holly's heroes

It's a rainy day, and there are gray clouds in the sky. Holly's walking to school. She has a history test. A lot of young people might feel unhappy or worried, but not Holly. Holly's just happy she can walk to school.
Last year, Holly was in the hospital for four weeks, and she had to learn to walk again. We ask Holly about her heroes.

So, Holly, can you tell us what happened to you last year?

I was riding my bike home from my friend's house after school. It was dark, and I didn't have any lights, so I couldn't see clearly. I was going very quickly down a hill close to our apartment, when a cat suddenly ran across the road in front of me. I tried not to hit it, but I fell off my bike.

How terrible! Then what happened?

Well, I can't remember. I hit my head because I wasn't wearing a helmet. People told me what happened. I fell badly and broke my leg in two places.

How did you get to the hospital?

A driver saw me on the ground and stopped his car. He called for an ambulance, and they took me to the nearest hospital. I arrived in less than ten minutes.

Wow! That was fast.

Yes. Thanks to them, the doctors and nurses could work quickly. I had an X-ray, and then they had to operate for four hours, but they saved my leg. Then I had to learn to walk again.

So you have a lot of heroes: the ambulance drivers and the team of doctors and nurses.

Yes, but also the driver who stopped to call the ambulance. I want to say thank you to everyone who helped me. When I grow up, I want to be a doctor or nurse because I'd like to help other people, too.

2 **75** **Listen and say "firefighter," "doctor," "police officer," or "ambulance driver."**

1 **Read and choose answers that are true for you.**

1 Your friend has a new haircut, and you think it looks awful. When he asks you what you think, you say:

a "It looks terrible. I don't like it."
b "It's OK, but I prefer the old haircut."
c "It looks amazing! It's perfect for you."

2 Your mom spent all afternoon making a special dinner, but you don't like it. What do you do?

a You eat it and ask for more.
b You make a horrible face and say you don't want to eat it.
c You tell her that it's nice, but it's not your favorite meal. You suggest a meal that she can make more quickly and easily.

3 You're shopping with a friend who wants to buy a new dress. She tries on a dress that looks awful on her. She asks you what you think. What do you do?

a You say the dress doesn't look very nice, and you find a different dress for her to try.
b You say that the dress looks great and tell her to buy it.
c You tell her the dress looks horrible and you're bored with shopping.

4 A new boy in your class invites you to play tennis on Saturday afternoon. You'd like to go to the movies with some friends. What do you do?

a You say, "Sorry, I can't. I want to go to the movies with my friends."
b You make a face and say, "I hate tennis!"
c You smile and say, "Thanks very much, but I want to go to the movies with some friends on Saturday. Would you like to come with us?"

5 You have a friend who sometimes smells bad after P.E. What's the best way to help him?

a Make a horrible face and say, "You smell bad. Take a shower!"
b Give him a box of shower gel and deodorant for his birthday.
c Talk about him with the other students and laugh.

6 Your dad doesn't have a job. He lost it last year, and your parents are worried about money. It's your birthday soon, and you want a big party, but your parents say that you can't have one this year. What do you do?

a You tell your parents that you understand and it isn't important.
b You get angry and stay in your room all day.
c You tell your parents that you understand. You ask your friends to bring some lemonade and snacks to the park so you can have a small party.

2 **Talk about your answers with a partner. Are they the same or different?**

3 **Discuss these questions.**

1 Why is it important to tell the truth?
2 What is trust and why is it important?
3 How can we tell our friends and family the truth and not hurt their feelings?

Units 7&8 Values **Value your friendships**

1 **Read the letters and answer the questions.**

Dear Betty and Robert,

I work really hard at school, and I always study a lot for my tests, but I don't get good grades. I don't fail, but I get 5, 6, or sometimes 7 out of 10.

My best friend, Emma, gets the best grades in the school, but she cheats. She takes pictures of the book on her cell phone and uses them during the tests. I'm really unhappy about this.

Should I do the same as my friend and get better grades, or should I tell the teacher that she cheats on tests? Please help me to decide.

Yours truly,

Nico

Dear Nico,

When you work hard in school and study for your tests, you are learning things. I'm sorry that you don't get the good grades that you want. But it's better to work hard and learn things than cheat and learn very little. It's not a good idea for you to do the same as Emma. You should feel good because you're passing your tests. Do your best and don't worry about other people's grades.

This situation is difficult. You don't have to tell the teacher that your friend is cheating. Emma can't always cheat — one day someone is going to catch her.

Yours truly,

Betty and Robert

1 Does Nico work hard at school?
2 Does he get good grades?
3 How does Emma cheat on the tests?
4 What do Betty and Robert think about cheating?
5 Do they think that Nico should get the same grades as other students?

 2 **Read the letter. Discuss these questions.**

1 Is Sarah right to be unhappy? Why?
2 What do you think Katya should do?
3 What do you think Sarah should do?

Dear Betty and Robert,

I'm really unhappy because I made a huge mistake with my best friend, Sarah. There's a group of very popular girls in my class. They're cool and funny, and everyone wants to be friends with them. They asked me to go out with them last Saturday. I was really excited, but it was Sarah's birthday.

I didn't go to Sarah's party, and now she's unhappy with me. She doesn't want to be my friend anymore. I've started to see that the popular girls are boring and mean, and I don't like going out with them. I want to be Sarah's best friend again. What should I do?

Yours truly,

Katya

Grammar reference

1

What time is it?

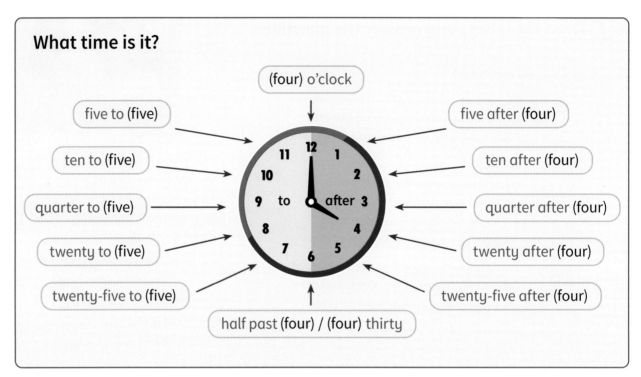

(four) o'clock

five to (five)
ten to (five)
quarter to (five)
twenty to (five)
twenty-five to (five)

five after (four)
ten after (four)
quarter after (four)
twenty after (four)
twenty-five after (four)

half past (four) / (four) thirty

2

We use *going to* to talk and write about the future.

Affirmative	Negative (n't = not)	Question
I'm going to work hard.	I'm not going to work hard.	Am I going to work hard?
She's going to work hard.	She isn't going to work hard.	Is she going to work hard?
They're going to work hard.	They aren't going to work hard.	Are they going to work hard?

3

right	↱	She turned right.
left	↰	They took the second street on the left.
across	↨	They looked and listened carefully before they walked across the street.
straight down	⇒	We walked straight down the street.
straight ahead	↰↑↱	He didn't turn. He drove straight ahead to the end of the road.
corner	↰	I turned at the corner.
past	▫↑	You have to walk past the park.

We use the past progressive to describe what was happening in the past.

Affirmative	Negative (n't = not)	Question
I was reading a book.	I wasn't reading a book.	Was I reading a book?
We were reading a book.	We weren't reading a book.	Were we reading a book?

We use *made of* to describe materials.

Affirmative	Negative (n't = not)	Question
It's made of metal.	It isn't made of metal.	Is it made of metal?
They're made of metal.	They aren't made of metal.	Are they made of metal?

We use verb + *like* to describe things.

Affirmative	Negative (n't = not)	Question
It sounds like a train.	It doesn't sound like a train.	Does it sound like a train?
They sound like cats.	They don't sound like cats.	Do they sound like cats?

We use *should* to give and ask for help or advice.

Affirmative	Negative (n't = not)	Question
I should tell my teacher.	I shouldn't tell my teacher.	Should I tell my teacher?
He should tell his teacher.	He shouldn't tell his teacher.	Should he tell his teacher?

We use the present perfect to talk and write about things we did at any time up to now.

Affirmative	Negative (n't = not)	Question
She's visited Seattle.	She hasn't visited Seattle.	Has she visited Seattle?
They've visited Seattle.	They haven't visited Seattle.	Have they visited Seattle?

Flyers Listening

1 🎧 76 **Describe the two pictures. Listen and circle A or B.**

Picture A

Picture B

1 A (B)

2 A B

3 A B

4 A B

5 A B

6 A B

2 🎧 77 🐵 **Listen and draw lines. There is one example.**

Betty William George Sophia

Holly Richard Oliver

A2 Flyers Exam folder: Listening Part 1

Flyers Listening

1 🎧 78 **Listen and draw arrows → ↑ ↗ .**

2 🎧 79 **Listen and mark (✓) the box. There is one example.**

When did Uncle David last see George?

A ☐   B ☐   C ✓

1 What's George's favorite subject?

A ☐   B ☐   C ☐

2 Which project is George doing at school now?

A ☐   B ☐   C ☐

3 Where did George go on his last field trip?

A ☐   B ☐   C ☐

4 Which instrument is Emma learning to play?

A ☐   B ☐   C ☐

5 What job does George want to do in the future?

A ☐   B ☐   C ☐

Flyers Listening

1 🎧 80 Talk about the differences. Listen and circle. Then complete the sentences.

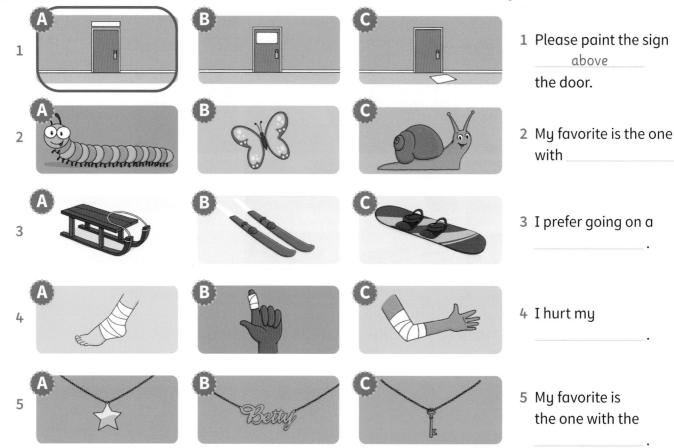

1 Please paint the sign <u>above</u> the door.

2 My favorite is the one with _____.

3 I prefer going on a _____.

4 I hurt my _____.

5 My favorite is the one with the _____.

2 🎧 81 🐵 Listen and color and write. There is one example.

HISTORY MUSEUM

Flyers Reading and Writing

1 Look. Use the code to color the squares.

passenger	ambulance	wood	sneakers	astronaut	wool
passenger	uniform	pilot	skiing	refrigerator	pajamas
rocket	bandage	golf	platform	airport	stove
station	oven	planet	medicine	glass	swimming

Key:

clothes = brown
space = yellow
air travel = blue
train travel = purple
sports = green
hospital = pink
kitchen = orange
materials = gray

2 Look and read. Choose the correct words and write them on the lines. There is one example.

a railway

pajamas

sneakers

a platform

a mechanic

envelopes

metal

a bridge

This person flies a plane and usually wears a uniform.	a pilot
1 People travel in cars down these large roads when they go on long trips.	
2 This is the name for a person who travels in a plane or taxi or on a train.	
3 People walk across this when they want to cross a road or river.	
4 You can stay in this when you are camping in the country.	
5 People usually wear these on their feet when they go running or play a sport.	
6 You can find these on coats and jackets. People put things like keys and money into them.	
7 This material comes from sheep, and people often use it to make sweaters.	
8 This person repairs cars and other machines.	
9 You walk down this in a station when you get on or off a train.	
10 You put letters inside these and write the addresses on the front.	

a pilot

pockets

stamps

a passenger

a tent

highways

wool

Flyers Reading and Writing

1 Read and guess the missing word. Is it a verb, singular noun, plural noun, adverb, or adjective?

1 My dad's not going to ___play (verb)___ golf today because it's windy. He says a ___storm (noun)___ is coming.

2 I didn't like sleeping in a _____. You can hear a lot of _____ animals at night.

3 There weren't many _____ on the train, so we sat next to the _____ and enjoyed the views.

4 We watched an _____ documentary last night about butterflies that _____ thousands of kilometers every winter.

5 My cousins _____ walking across the bridge when they saw dolphins in the _____ .

6 Yesterday my sister and I made a _____ cake, but we forgot to add sugar! It wasn't very _____ !

2 Read the story. Choose a word from the box. Write the correct word next to numbers 1–5. There is one example.

~~competition~~   friendly   already   new   invitation   filmed   time   exciting   date   wrote

Last night, when Oliver and Sophia were leaving the movie theater, they saw a poster about a music ___competition___ . The producer of a famous TV music show was looking for a young rock band to be in a (**1**) _____ film. They had to send a video to the email address on the poster.

Oliver and Sophia were in a band. Oliver played the piano, Sophia was the singer, and the other two members, Harry and Emma, played the guitar.

Oliver showed them the poster on his phone at school the next day. "But look at the (**2**) _____ !" said Harry. "We need to send the video before April 17. That's tomorrow!"

"Let's make a video of our new song, 'Foggy Days,' right now," said Emma.

Sophia's brother borrowed his dad's camera. He (**3**) _____ the band on the school stage and emailed the video after school. A month later, they found out that their song didn't win. They were all unhappy, but Emma said, "It doesn't matter, our band is (**4**) _____ famous at school!"

The next day, a different TV producer called Emma. "I'd like to play your song at the beginning of our weather forecast," he said, "When it's foggy, of course!"

"Wow!" laughed Oliver. "That's (**5**) _____ news!" Everyone agreed.

(6) **Now choose the best name for the story. Mark (✓) one box.**

☐ A special music video   ☐ A song on TV

☐ Rock band winners!

Flyers Reading and Writing

1 **Read and complete so the two sentences have the same meaning. You can use 1, 2, 3, or 4 words.**

1 Sarah really didn't like storms because she was scared of lightning.

    <u> Lightning </u> frightened Sarah.

2 One night when Yuna was camping with her family, there was a strange sound and she got up.

    Yuna got up when she heard a _____ .

3 Kito and his family were happy when they put their groceries in the car and drove home.

    The family went home happily after they had _____ in the car.

2 🐵 **Look at the picture and read the story. Write some words to complete the sentences about the story. You can use 1, 2, 3, or 4 words.**

The students in Class 6A were excited as they woke up on the first morning of their school ski trip. They all got dressed and hurried to have breakfast as fast as they could. The mountains around the hotel looked amazing.

"What time do the skiing classes start?" asked Robert. "It's going to be so much fun!"

Their teacher, Mrs. West, looked worried but smiled and said, "I have some bad news and some good news."

The bad news was that there was no skiing for the first three days because the snow was too deep. But the good news was that a pair of eagles was making their nest between some rocks on the highest mountain. Many people thought this kind of eagle was extinct.

"There cannot not be any activity on the mountains at this time," Mrs. West explained, "but we can do a project about eagles instead."

"We studied extinct animals in our science class, and it was really interesting," said Robert.

The students were also happy when they found out that there was ice on a lake behind the hotel, so everyone could take ice-skating classes for three days.

"It was funny when we actually started our skiing classes," Helen told her mom when she was back home. "We kept falling all the time because we were watching the eagles flying above us!"

Examples

It was the first day of the students' <u> ski trip </u> .

The students wanted to eat <u> breakfast </u> quickly.

Questions

1 The students could see _____ outside the hotel.

2 The teacher told them they couldn't go _____ for several days.

3 She also told them some _____ about eagles.

4 The nests weren't easy to see because they were high up _____ .

5 The students already knew about _____ from their science class.

6 The students were happy they could go _____ on the lake.

7 Many students looked up at the eagles during their skiing classes and _____ a lot.

Flyers Speaking

1 🎧 82 **Listen and circle the differences in picture 2. Then listen and complete the sentences about picture 1.**

Picture 1   Picture 2

In picture 1, …

1 two children are ___making a fire___ .
2 a man in the stream is _____ of two butterflies.
3 a girl is _____ the bridge.
4 the boy's _____ are in his backpack.
5 there are _____ and a path.
6 a boy is _____ under a tree.

2 🎧 83 🐵 **Listen. Talk about the differences. Listen again to check your answers.**

Flyers Speaking

1 **Look at the picture. Ask and answer with a partner.**

Where / castle?   Where / mom and daughter go?   Who / walk dog?   What time?

How many children / get on bus?   What old woman / pull?   What girl / read?

Sunny or foggy?

2 🎧 84 🙂 **Listen. Answer the questions about William's trip. Then ask questions about Katy's trip.**

William's trip	
Where / going	Westfield
How / travel	bus
What time / leave	10:30
Who / visit	grandmother
City / Country	the country

Katy's trip	
Where / going	?
How / travel	?
What time / leave	?
Who / visit	?
City / Country	?

Thanks and Acknowledgments

Authors' thanks

Many thanks to everyone at Cambridge University Press & Assessment for their dedication and hard work, and in particular to:

Louise Wood for doing such a great job overseeing the level; Catriona Brownlee for her dedication and sound editorial judgment; freelance editors Melissa Bryant and Sarah Jane Lewis.

We would also like to thank all our students and colleagues, past, present, and future, at Star English academy in Murcia, especially Jim Kelly for his friendship and support throughout the years.

Dedications

To Jim Kelly: Here's to the next thirty years of our Starship enterprise. – CN

To my Murcian family: Adolfo and Isabel, the Peinado sisters and their other halves for always treating me so well, thanks for being there and for making my life in Murcia so much fun. – MT

Illustrations

Antonio Cuesta; Dave Williams, Ana Sebastian (Bright Agency); David Belmont, Javier Joaquin, Laszlo Veres, Moreno Chiacchiera (Beehive); Shahab (Sylvie Poggio Artists).

Audio

Audio production by John Marshall Media.

Video

Video acknowledgments are in the Teacher Resources on Cambridge One.

Design and typeset

Blooberry Design

Additional authors

Rebecca Legros and Robin Thompson (CLIL); Montse Watkin (Sounds and life skills, Exam folder)

The authors and publishers acknowledge the following sources of copyright material and are grateful for the permissions granted. While every effort has been made, it has not always been possible to identify the sources of all the material used, or to trace all copyright holders. If any omissions are brought to our notice, we will be happy to include the appropriate acknowledgments on reprinting and in the next update to the digital edition, as applicable.

Key: U = Unit, R = Review, V = Values

Photography

All the photos are sourced from Getty Images.

U0: Compassionate Eye Foundation/Martin Barraud/Stone; teekid/E+; mediaphotos/iStock/Getty Images Plus; Ableimages/DigitalVision; FatCamera/E+; Monty Rakusen/Image Source; ullstein bild; PhotoMelon/iStock/Getty Images Plus; Martin Barraud/Stone; iLexx/iStock/Getty Images Plus; AndreaAstes/iStock/Getty Images Plus; Brennan Bucannan/EyeEm; Print Collector/Hulton Archive; allanswart/iStock/Getty Images; Roman Bykhalets/iStock/Getty Images Plus; SMSka/iStock/Getty Images Plus; MsMoloko/iStock/Getty Images Plus; U1: ZargonDesign/E+; metamorworks/iStock/Getty Images Plus; all images copyright of Jamie Lamb - elusive-images.co.uk/Moment; Dmytro Aksonov/E+; CBS Photo Archive; simonkr/E+; Tony Garcia/Image Source; Marc Dufresne/E+; pigphoto/iStock/Getty Images Plus; angie marie photography/Moment; EXTREME-PHOTOGRAPHER/iStock/Getty Images Plus; Richard Newstead/Moment; Mark Stevenson/Stocktrek Images; Reinhard Dirscherl/The Image Bank; Dgwildlife/iStock/Getty Images Plus; FARBAI/iStock/Getty Images Plus; U2: monkeybusinessimages/iStock/Getty Images Plus; FatCamera/iStock/Getty Images Plus; Mahmud013/E+; Guy Cali/Corbis; Maskot; Erik Isakson/Tetra images; miodrag ignjatovic/E+; AleksandarNakic/E+; David Madison/Stone; adoc-photos/Corbis Historical; Aitor Alcalde Colomer/Getty Images Sport; Larry Marano/Getty Images Entertainment; Kent Nishimura/Los Angeles Times; Bloomberg; filmstudio/E+; sinology/Moment; Lacheev/iStock/Getty Images Plus; Yellow Dog Productions/The Image Bank; Westend61; Somyot Techapuwapat/Moment; Jose A. Bernat Bacete/Moment; PATRICK T. FALLON/AFP; CZQS2000/STS/Photodisc; Peter Dazeley/The Image Bank; Chonticha Vatpongpee/EyeEm; Jose A. Bernat Bacete/Moment; syntika/iStock/Getty Images Plus; eyewave/iStock/Getty Images Plus; U3: SOPA Images/LightRocket; _ultraforma_/iStock Unreleased; Andrea Pistolesi/Stone; Sara Amroussi/EyeEm; Sergio Amiti/Moment; aapsky/iStock/Getty Images Plus; Vladislav Zolotov/iStock/Getty Images Plus; BaMa/Photographer's Choice RF; Cris Cantᴬ³n/Moment; DANNY HU/Moment; Â© Allard Schager/Moment; Blake Callahan/Moment; Hiroshi Higuchi/The Image Bank Unreleased; Caroline Purser/The Image Bank; SERGII IAREMENKO/SCIENCE PHOTO LIBRARY/Science Photo Library; aleksei-veprev/iStock/Getty Images Plus; LisLud/iStock/Getty Images Plus; U4: Aaron Foster/The Image Bank; omgimages/iStock/Getty Images Plus; Jamie Grill/The Image Bank; Design Pics/Ron Nickel; Tempura/E+; Ascent Xmedia/Stone; Imgorthand/

E+; Neustockimages/E+; Jeff Greenough/Tetra images; John Parrot/Stocktrek Images; Historical/Corbis Historical; Juanmonino/E+; Westend61; Haje Jan Kamps/EyeEm; shannonstent/E+; Matt Anderson Photography/Moment; MARK GARLICK/SCIENCE PHOTO LIBRARY; RomanKhomlyak/iStock/Getty Images Plus; James L. Amos/Corbis Documentary; Roc Canals/Moment; Anna Sviridenko/iStock/Getty Images Plus; Lucie Kasparova/iStock/Getty Images Plus; U5: StratosGiannikos/iStock/Getty Images Plus; iakovenko/iStock/Getty Images Plus; artefy/iStock/Getty Images Plus; Smith Chetanachan/EyeEm; malerapaso/iStock/Getty Images Plus; Jena Ardell/Moment; Aleksandr Zubkov/Moment; DonNichols/E+; benedek/E+; Rajanish Kakade/AP; Daniel_M/iStock/Getty Images Plus; AFP; Marina Inoue/Moment; Jamroen Jaiman/EyeEm; J_rg Lcking/EyeEm; ThomasVogel/E+; Nattapol Sritongcom/EyeEm; IlexImage/E+; Jurgita Vaicikeviciene/EyeEm; Mohamad Faizal Ramli/EyeEm; malerapaso/E+; Wong Sze Fei/EyeEm; WYSIWYG/500px; fotoember/iStock Editorial; Michael Roberts/Moment Unreleased; Education Images/Universal Images Group; Paul Biris/Moment Open; Justin Case/The Image Bank; noppadon_sangpeam/iStock/Getty Images Plus; ExpressIPhoto/iStock/Getty Images Plus; Fajar Pramudianto/iStock/Getty Images Plus; Floortje/iStock/Getty Images Plus U6: Nikola Vukicevic/iStock/Getty Images Plus; Xvision/Moment; Elena Levchenko/EyeEm; Paolo Cordoni/EyeEm; Richard Sharrocks/Moment; Andrea La Civita/EyeEm; Westend61; Nitat Termmee/Moment; piranka/E+; Dorling Kindersley/Dorling Kindersley RF; Tom-Kichi/iStock/Getty Images Plus; Peter Cade/Stone; George Karbus Photography/Image Source; John Short/Design Pics; Images By Tang Ming Tung/DigitalVision; REDA\u0026CO/Universal Images Group; SENRYU/iStock/Getty Images Plus; U7: George Pachantouris/Moment; Seamind Panadda/EyeEm; Picture by Tambako the Jaguar/Moment; EcoPic/iStock/Getty Images Plus; Ed Reschke/Stone; Jasius/Moment; Ceneri/DigitalVision Vectors; Tim Grist Photography/Moment; Jordan Lye/Moment; FotoDuets/iStock/Getty Images Plus; Dimijana/iStock/Getty Images Plus; Voyagerix/iStock/Getty Images Plus; bradleym/E+; elenabs/iStock/Getty Images Plus; AlexeyBlogoodf/iStock/Getty Images Plus; Ekaterina Bedoeva/iStock/Getty Images Plus; Dawid Lech/foap; Nataliia Korzina/EyeEm; USO/iStock/Getty Images Plus; Linda Krueger/500Px Plus; schnuddel/E+; porojnicu/iStock/Getty Images Plus; Trudie Davidson/Moment; U8: DieterMeyrl/E+; Janie Airey/Image Source; sonyae/iStock/Getty Images Plus; mbbirdy/E+; pyotr021/iStock/Getty Images Plus; Imgorthand/E+; Cavan Images; Blend Images - Erik Isakson/Tetra images; SDI Productions/E+; triloks/E+; sot/Photodisc; Â© Marco Bottigelli/Moment; Westend61/Brand X Pictures; FatCamera/E+; quavondo/E+; cjp/E+; luplupme/iStock/Getty Images Plus; Kai-Otto Melau/Getty Images Sport; Hirurg/E+; Augustas Cetkauskas/EyeEm; Jason Hosking/Corbis; R12: izusek/iStock/Getty Images Plus; R34: David Goddard/Getty Images News; P A Thompson/The Image Bank; Jose Luis Pelaez Inc/DigitalVision; R56: Nikada/E+; Zoonar RF; DNY59/E+; Peerayot/iStock/Getty Images Plus; Vasko/E+; AlexandrMoroz/iStock/Getty Images Plus; Nattawut Lakjit/EyeEm; lunglee/iStock/Getty Images Plus; yorkfoto/iStock/Getty Images Plus; Gorlov/iStock/Getty Images Plus; R.Tsubin/Moment; Sjo/E+; Mika Mika/Moment; Alex Savochkin/500px; Suradech14/iStock/Getty Images Plus; Peter Dazeley/The Image Bank; Yevgen Romanenko/Moment; dashu83/iStock/Getty Images Plus; Jamroen Jaiman/EyeEm; Adha Ghazali/EyeEm; Athitat Shinagowin/EyeEm; evemilla/E+; LauriPatterson/iStock/Getty Images Plus; bortonia/E+; Issarawat Tattong/Moment; gdagys/E+; -MG-/E+; zhongyanjiang/iStock/Getty Images Plus; Ociacia/iStock/Getty Images Plus; TanyaRozhnovskaya/iStock/Getty Images Plus; Eskay Lim/EyeEm; koto_feja/iStock/Getty Images Plus; Riddy/iStock/Getty Images Plus; JohnGollop/iStock/Getty Images Plus; rudchenko/iStock/Getty Images Plus; Jamesmcq24/E+; Sittichai Karimpard/EyeEm; R78: Glowimages; Brockswood/iStock/Getty Images Plus; benimage/E+; subjug/iStock/Getty Images Plus; Cavan Images/iStock/Getty Images Plus; Cimmerian/E+; pagadesign/E+; Tetra Images/Tetra images; Kyrylo Glivin/EyeEm; Caspar Benson/fStop; shunli zhao/Moment; Jose Luis Pelaez Inc/DigitalVision; artpipi/E+; sound35/iStock/Getty Images Plus; Talaj/iStock/Getty Images Plus; vauvau/iStock/Getty Images Plus; Gannet77/E+; Hill Street Studios/DigitalVision; Iurii Korolev/iStock/Getty Images Plus; onurdongel/iStock/Getty Images Plus; luoman/E+; powerofforever/iStock/Getty Images Plus; V34: Gary John Norman/DigitalVision; V78: Sam Edwards/OJO Images; FARBAI/iStock/Getty Images Plus; EF: FamVeld/iStock/Getty Images Plus; Nahhan/iStock/Getty Images Plus; Empato/E+; Prasit photo/Moment; jsmith/iStock/Getty Images Plus; CreativeNature_nl/iStock/Getty Images Plus; Andrew Holt/The Image Bank; Jovo Marjanovic/EyeEm; MR1805/iStock/Getty Images Plus; Digital Zoo/DigitalVision; Peter Rahm/EyeEm; Serkan Erol/EyeEm; Sergio Amiti/Moment; Turnervisual/E+; d3sign/Moment; Mike Kemp/Tetra images; Â© Marco Bottigelli/Moment; Imgorthand/E+; Hanna Shyriaieva/iStock/Getty Images Plus; Kyle Lee/EyeEm.

The following photographs are sourced from other sources/libraries.

U1: Pictorial Press Ltd/Alamy Stock Photo; U2: Luciano Cosmo/Shutterstock; U4: Andrea Danti/Shutterstock; U7: Matthijs Kuijpers/Alamy Stock Photo; U8: Ian Middleton/Alamy Stock Photo.

Cover photography by Tiffany Mumford for Creative Listening.

Commissioned photography by Stephen Noble and Duncan Yeldham for Creative Listening.